The Salt Lake Papers

The Salt Lake Papers
From the Years in the Earthscapes of Utah

EDWARD LUEDERS

THE UNIVERSITY OF UTAH PRESS
Salt Lake City

The Defiance House Man colophon is a registered trademark of
The University of Utah Press. It is based on a four-foot-tall Ancient
Puebloan pictograph (late PIII) near Glen Canyon, Utah.

LIBRARY OF CONGRESS CATALOGING-IN-PUBLICATION DATA
Names: Lueders, Edward, 1923- author.
Title: The Salt Lake papers : from the years in the earthscapes of Utah /
    Edward Lueders.
Description: Salt Lake City : The University of Utah Press, [2018] |
    Identifiers: LCCN 2018002470 (print) | LCCN 2018005899 (ebook) | ISBN
    9781607816362 () | ISBN 9781607816355 | ISBN 9781607816355?q(pbk.)
Subjects: LCSH: Lueders, Edward, 1923---Homes and haunts--Utah. | Authors,
    American--20th century--Diaries. | Natural history--Utah--Great Salt Lake.
    | Natural history--Colorado Plateau.
Classification: LCC PS3562.U34 (ebook) | LCC PS3562.U34 Z465 2018 (print) |
    DDC 818/.5403 [B] --dc23
LC record available at https://lccn.loc.gov/2018002470

Printed and bound in the United States of America.

ONCE AGAIN FOR JOEL

And for all my students, whoever, wherever, whenever they be

BOOKS BY EDWARD LUEDERS

Through Okinawan Eyes, edited with Jane Kluckhohn. University of New Mexico Press, 1951.

Carl Van Vechten and the Twenties. University of New Mexico Press, 1955.

Carl Van Vechten. Twayne, 1965.

Reflections on a Gift of Watermelon Pickle, edited with Stephen Dunning and Hugh Smith. Scott Foresman, 1966.

Some Haystacks Don't Have Any Needle, edited with Stephen Dunning and Hugh Smith. Scott Foresman, 1969.

Zero Makes Me Hungry, edited with Primus St. John. Scott Foresman, 1976.

The Clam Lake Papers. Harper & Row, 1977 .

The Wake of the General Bliss. University of Utah Press, 1989.

Writing Natural History: Dialogue with Authors (editor). University of Utah Press, 1989.

Like Underground Water: The Poetry of Mid-Twentieth Century Japan. Translated with Naoshi Koriyama. Copper Canyon Press, 1995.

CONTENTS

PREFACE   ix

BOOK ONE: *Salt Lake City and the Great Salt Lake*

Prologue   3

The Papers (from the 1980s)   11

Epilogue: The Hawaii Episode   59

BOOK TWO: *Torrey, the Colorado Plateau, and the Colorado River*

Prologue   65

The Papers   69

Epilogue: The Disquisition: On Language, Number, and the Humanities: An Epistemology for the Digital Age   103

PREFACE

I have tried in this contemplative book, as I did fashioning *The Clam Lake Papers* fifty years ago, to meld my observations in a continuity of thought and place, as conscious of the physical environment I inhabit and feel myself a part of as in the train and thrust of the thought that it provokes. As a result, this book falls naturally into two composite parts in both time and place.

It will be important for the reader to know that BOOK ONE was actually researched, written, and compiled in the 1980s, during the years following my move from the Midwest to Salt Lake City, Utah. There, it was the mountain and high-desert geological landscapes that helped to re-direct and lengthen my thought. My aquarian affinities had shifted from the inter-connected freshwater Great Lakes and the seasonal environment of Clam Lake, Wisconsin, to the singular, isolate, "dead" inland sea of the Great Salt Lake, into which all inflow is held without further drainage, complete in itself with the accumulation of its mineral "salts" held in suspension.

These "Salt Lake Papers" presented here as BOOK ONE, having been set aside in the late 1980s in favor of more timely grant-funded projects, have also been held in suspension. They have been unpublished until now, when I find that they have awaited their role here as tokens of my personal, geophysical, and intellectual history from the late decades of the twentieth century, suitable to my current perspectives and purposes, as well as to their own. They appear virtually un-altered and un-edited here after some thirty years of lying in wait.

BOOK TWO was written following my subsequent move to the home my wife and I built on an open mesa near Torrey, Utah, near Capitol Reef National Park and the geological landscapes of the sparsely populated Colorado Plateau. There, the mountains and high-desert land are continuously drained and shaped by the accumulation of tributaries into and through the Colorado River, eventually—if any water is left after diversion and irrigation for human uses—into the Sea of Cortez and thus to the Pacific and the oceans of the world.

The sequence from Torrey is a series of confluences beginning with the Fremont River (flowing from the mountain basin of Fish Lake and a series of small reservoirs) to confluences past Torrey with Sulphur and Sand Creeks, then with Muddy Creek from the San Rafael Swell drainage, then the Dirty Devil, and then, along with the Little Colorado from the east, to the major confluence with the Green River, gathered from Idaho, Colorado, Wyoming, and Utah to merge in Canyonlands National Park, with its dammed impoundment following in Utah's Lake Powell and, again, in Lake Mead at the Nevada border, after the meanders and whitewater rapids through Grand Canyon in Arizona.

In consequence, my thought in BOOK TWO is fashioned from that environment, shaped by 360 degrees of Earth horizon and the erosion of the surrounding land laid bare by eons of abrasive water drainage, seasonal freeze-and-thaw, and abrasive weather and wind.

Because human thought is abstracted from the processing of human experience, it tends to be a distraction from the living instance and the concerns of physical immediacy. Thus, the tendency of philosophical speculation is always to move away from matters at hand, the current actualities of place and time—all the aspects of environment in which the thought takes place.

I hope to think with the crux of my thought through my feet on the ground, as well as my head in the air. And, as I draft these papers, this now takes place amid the prodigious twenty-first-century technological environment of the binary advance into what we've named the Digital Age.

The historians John Wesley Powell in the nineteenth century and Wallace Stegner in the twentieth century, both of whom explored and knew personally the geography of the American Southwest, prophesied accurately that its future growth, development, and welfare would depend on our use of its scant native supply of water. I trust that, along with their probable surprise, they each would approve of both my physical and my metaphysical uses of Utah's two distinctive hydrological drainages—one from the populous Wasatch Front in the north into the natural impoundment of Great Salt Lake, and the other from the confluence of tributaries draining the Colorado Plateau in the south through the Colorado River. These drainages serve metaphorically—as the astute reader will discern—as both scene and symbol throughout the two-in-one book that follows.

Eventually, BOOK TWO leads to its epilogue in the formal disquisition "On Language, Number, and the Humanities: An Epistemology for the Digital Age," with considerations of basic and broader pertinence to human beings living on Earth in the twenty-first-century worlds of naming, nature, and number.

BOOK ONE

Salt Lake City and the Great Salt Lake

PROLOGUE

I was born inland from the shores of Lake Michigan on the north side of Chicago, and I was "raised" as a midwesterner. For much of my life, therefore, I naturally calculated my days, months, years wholly by the calendar and the round of seasons.

A common expression we had—this one a bit literary—reflects this way of signaling age and the passage of one's lifetime. "A youth of so many summers," we'd say. Or, more fittingly as the cycles of seasons and one's age advance, "of so many winters."

But there in Chicago through those summers, as one long humid day would melt into the next, I forgot to count. In the midwestern summers of my youth, everything unfurled and expanded during its season under the sun.

By mid-June, the trees and gardens and small rectangular patches of grass in the yards of my north-side Chicago neighborhood flourished. Magically, the rigid grid-work of the city was softened. Irrepressible green weeds forced their way up through the slightest cracks in the concrete sidewalks and alleyways that I roamed through the summers of my childhood.

By mid-July, the oversized empty lot along Lincoln Avenue near our house was a tangle of whiskery green stalks, dusty leaves, and towering ragweed tassels, as tall as I was and taller—high and thick enough to make a private summer world in which to hide from the surrounding city. Quite unaware of any historical perspective in our midwestern vocabulary, we called that empty lot "the prairie." Whether I was hiding, digging, moving through, or just languishing

in the thick summer growth of "the prairie" in my innocent, unin-
structed child's play, I can remember feeling part human, part animal,
part insect, part plant—very much what I would now call organic.

Even in our big city neighborhood, trees in full leaf shielded us
from the midsummer sun. Quite on their own, the indestructible
so-called trees of heaven—also called "stink trees" by some—sprang
up everywhere, growing to tree size in a single season, even in oil-
soaked, gravel-and-cinder parking spaces, where apartment dwellers
parked their cars. We would snap off the fast-growing spur branches,
strip them of their pointed, opposite-growing leaves, and use them
as play whips.

Elm, oak, and maple trees of varying size and spread shaded yards
and lined the side streets between the sidewalks and pavement. One
nearby residential block was graced on both sides of the street by
enormous, soaring, overarching ancient elms, which made a vaulted
canopy of green all summer and provided a home for countless birds
and colonies of scampering gray squirrels. Bird block, we called it. We
would ride our scooters or roller skates over there to watch the flash-
ing avian world in its branches and listen to the varieties of songbirds
to be heard above and behind the raucous scolding of blue jays and
the cawing of occasional crows.

The neighborhood I grew up in was called Ravenswood. It was a
compound term I took altogether for granted as given in my child's
world—like *lakemichigan*, *chicago-illinoy*, *downtown*, *heatlightning*,
snapdragon, *butterfly*, or my own self-contained name, *edwerdleed-
erz*. It took many summers and winters before, looking back, I realized what the name Ravenswood meant, how it must have come
to be, and what it said about those venerable trees in the cityscape I
was born in.

My father was an avid fisherman. It followed that the family's vacations were directed northward, beyond the cultivated cornfields of
Illinois, through the rolling hills and dairy farms of southern Wisconsin, to the bass and muskellunge waters of Manitowish and Lac

du Flambeau. Eventually, we had our own family summer place near
Clam Lake, Wisconsin, over four hundred miles northwest of Chicago, deep in the heart of the Chequamegon National Forest. I knew
only green, lush summers then, full and expansive summers, whether
in the rich, black loam of Illinois Midwest farmlands or in the North-
woods cover of Wisconsin's glacial carvings and deposits above the
Precambrian shield of the western Great Lakes.

Later on, I was to think a good deal about winter in the seasonal
rounds of that still remote Clam Lake country. But that led to another book than the one I mean to introduce here. I am only an occasional visitor to those midwestern locales of my youth these days.

For the second half of my life, I have lived in the open, mercilessly
exposed landscapes of the high desert and Intermountain West—in
particular, I made my home in the Salt Lake Valley of northern Utah.

My first Salt Lake City house was situated above and southeast
of the city, partway up the foothills of the Wasatch Range that rise
up to 10,000- and 11,000-foot peaks over my shoulder. The house
was built on what is known locally as a "bench"—a term for one of
the still-visible former shorelines of the prehistoric inland sea geog-
raphers have named Lake Bonneville, which covered an enormous
area of the Great Basin stretching from the Wasatch Range west and
northwest into what we now call Nevada and Idaho. The shoreline
of that ancient Lake Bonneville reached its highest level some fourteen thousand to sixteen thousand years ago, near the end of its glacial epoch—the most recent of the so-called ice ages the Great Basin
has gone through.

The front deck of that house, cantilevered past the surrounding thicket of native Gambel oak, looked out over a scalloped patch
of lawn that fell away to an impressive view across the twenty-mile-
wide Salt Lake Valley. Along the horizon to the northwest lay a wide
strip of water, the color of which varied with the prevailing Utah skies
from deep blue to slate gray. This is what remains of the ancient Lake
Bonneville. In our time it is the namesake of the burgeoning city that

buzzes and hums with urban growth and activity between it and me: it is the Great Salt Lake of Utah.

Although reduced to a remnant of the enormous inland sea that was Lake Bonneville, this exotic, barren, apparently lifeless expanse of water is still imposing in its spread of nearly seventy-five miles from south to north.

To a considerable extent, Great Salt Lake presided over my life in the Intermountain West. It has become a repository, as both fact and symbol, for the perspectives that have developed with my view from the east bench. With the rugged Wasatch Range at my back to the east, I looked out over the teeming grid-work of Brigham Young's city—a mere hundred and seventy-odd years after that enterprising Mormon leader arrived with his band of intrepid pioneers and began at once diverting the mountain streams into irrigation ditches— streams that continue to drain the rugged lands on all sides into that strange, unlikely body of salt water on the horizon, from which there is no outlet.

From the shores of Lake Michigan, that gigantic freshwater glacial scoop of the northern Midwest, to the benches of prehistoric Lake Bonneville; from the birch and evergreen woods, the reed and lily-pad shorelines, and the partially spring-fed, muskie-weed depths of Clam Lake, Wisconsin, to the stark margins and inhospitable brine of Utah's Great Salt Lake, six times saltier than the oceans of the world; I find that I am not so much an uprooted midwesterner as I am a transplanted aquarian—transplanted in time as well as place, affected by the perennial flow and impounding of water, instructed as a human observer by the life and look of this dramatic, graphic land, and by our expanding ability to read and interpret the geomorphic stories it has to tell.

Some years ago, when my cousin, Leonard DeMichele, was visiting in Utah, I took him to see the Great Salt Lake. Len has lived all his life in Chicago and its northern suburbs and a second home in Florida, but he has travelled a fair amount, has been to Europe, and has toured many of the popular vacation routes around the US by car—is himself a dealer in cars and the distribution of their parts. In Utah he was eager to add the Great Salt Lake to his list of sights, and I was pleased to oblige.

We drove north from the city to the town of Syracuse and then over the gravel causeway—at that time well above the water—which connected the eastern shoreline of the Lake with the largely uninhabited Antelope Island. Once on the island we continued over a dirt road that rose gradually for a few miles to the base of a peninsular prominence on the west face of the island. At the end of the road was a turnaround, where we parked and got out. From there I led Len over a steep half-mile trail that ended on the rocky ledge of a promontory that angled down, rather abruptly but not dangerously, to the spreading surface of the Lake some three or four hundred feet below. We sat on this rock and rested from the exertion of the hike, speaking briefly of our awe as we gazed out over the astonishing view the ledge commanded.

It was a clear, bright day in late April. The expanse of Great Salt Lake and the barrenness of its setting were laid out almost endlessly before us. From that height, the Lake looked slightly wrinkled by the spring breezes playing across it. Under the midday sun, over wide stretches of its rich reflection of open blue sky, the surface danced with diamond-bright sparkles and glitter.

We ceased talking and stood up to survey the extraordinary panorama. To our left the stretch of glistening blue water was interrupted only by the distant rise of the Oquirrh Range and the Stansbury Mountains twenty to thirty miles to the south and southwest. Looking straight across, we could scan some twenty miles of salt sea before it gave way to the dun-gray salt flats and the rise of distant ridges across the horizon of basin-and-range landforms westward into Nevada. The view to our right left no doubt that we stood before a great shimmering inland sea. Northward, both shorelines grew gradually remote and indistinct in the distance following the march of the Wasatch Range to the northeast and the intermittent low, barren ridgelines to the northwest. In the vast expanse between these dwindling lines of perspective was the spreading, crystalline, almost metallic blue surface of the Great Salt Lake as far as the eye could see, to the horizon and beyond, where the flat-map model in my head told me lay the state of Idaho and then the international boundary, Alberta, the Canadian Rockies, the arctic circle, the north polar cap.

Behind us, effectively blocking out everything but the open sky riding over it, rose the bulk of Antelope Island. Apparently, we two were alone on the island that weekday morning. Nothing—not even our car, hidden behind and below the rocks we had climbed over to reach our overlook—nothing of the civilized world intruded. I glanced over my shoulder, checking my bearings, curious to locate myself in relation to any familiar landmarks—that is, people-marks—in or around the bustling city we'd left behind. But we were sealed off. Only in my imagination could I visualize the busy sprawl of the Wasatch Front, its preoccupations and tentacles hidden behind the long spine of the island rising behind us. I searched the sky for the telltale pall and stain from the Kennecott smelter at the south end of the Lake, looking in vain for the towering stacks topping the blast furnaces whose smoke usually spewed into the ambient air. Evidently they were in temporary lull or remission, for nothing showed. I turned back, elated in my enveloping sense of pure isolation, to survey the great reaches of salt water again.

For an unbroken, soundless, continuous interlude, I felt the fullness of unencumbered time, participating in the sunlit vitality that animated the enormous land- and water-scape before me. The air was sharp and sweet in my nostrils, clean as I took it deep into my lungs.

Len and I had long since run out of our small conversation. Silence had taken us over—the enormous, complete, eloquent, singing silence of the far-reaching scene we were in. It was full of music for me rather than voices—music in my being rather than in my ears, sweeter and dearer music, as Keats intimates in his ode, for being unheard.

The midwestern voice of my cousin from Chicago broke into my reverie. "Where are the people?" he had asked. A note of small panic was in the tone of his question.

"People?" I repeated. "What people?"

"Anybody," he said. "Just…people. There aren't any people. There's no sign of any people."

I shrugged.

"It's so quiet," he said. "I never heard anything so quiet," he added with a short laugh. But it was a nervous laugh. I looked in his face and saw genuine bewilderment.

"It's too quiet," he decided. "How can there be all this" (he gestured broadly over the Great Salt Lake, out to the distant horizons) "and no people?"

He was clearly uncomfortable, uncomprehending, and somehow threatened. Emerging from the spell of my own preoccupation, I realized how alien he felt, how dispossessed he found himself in what was for him this totally barren landscape without semblance or hint of anything human other than our insignificant selves perched on that dizzying overlook. It was a kind of reverse culture shock for him. For perhaps the first time in his life he found himself wrapped in a total landscape quite unmarked by and apparently wholly indifferent to anything human—and thus to him. He literally was lost. He didn't know where he was. It was as if he stood on some unknown, uninhabited, lifeless moon.

He shook his head good-naturedly, but he was frowning. I could think of nothing further to say, no way to assuage his uneasiness. Not wishing, myself, to break into the continuing expansive silence of the scene, I didn't speak. Instead, I swept one more long look out over that marvelous, severe, unconcerned yet ultimately forgiving landscape, absorbing as much as I could of the scintillating glitter from its mineral-heavy water. Then I shrugged again, smiled, gestured over my shoulder with my head, and started back to the car.

THE PAPERS
(FROM THE 1980s)

The striking blue-green or aqua color of lakes and streams in the high North American Rocky Mountains is caused by what is called glacial *flour*, the powdered stone, ground dust-fine by the action of the glaciers in the slow friction of their inexorable movement. The effect is similar to the salts and minerals deposited and held in suspension in the Great Salt Lake of northern Utah, which at certain times, seen under strong light, has its own striking greens and blues. But they seem, somehow, naturally metallic.

~

The engineer says, "Give me men to move my mountains."

The student of Earth says, "The mountains, in their own time, are always moving, always being moved."

The preacher, invoking subservience to his God, says, "Faith can move mountains."

Dwarfed by a sublime mountain scene, the tourist is moved by the experience. Then, reducing it to his terms, he renders it inert through the rectangular frame of his camera.

The poet of love, struggling against the inertia of mere facts, seeking to match with words the ecstasy of the orgasmic moment when physical being blends in a wholeness of spirit with the beloved, reaches for a metaphor that might link the moment with the largeness of all time, all experience, all wonder. "Ah," he cries, "the earth moved!"

In the privacy of their passion, the man, aware suddenly of outbreak in the emotional tumult of his loved one, whether the source of her tears be distress or the excess of joy, relinquishes his own disquiet to assuage hers. Still the lover, he becomes the Father. Romantic love becomes care and assurance. Inevitabilities become personal, integrated with his love. "It's all right," he says, "I'm here."

The woman, recognizing cresting emotional tumult in her loved one, sensing the congestion of his unwept tears, puts aside her own. More than ever his lover, she becomes Mother. Love becomes consolation and the perpetuation of all connection. She locates the center of human life in a minding of the affections, of continuance in the face of affliction, of excess itself, through love. "It's all right," she says, "I'm here."

Mother Nature and Father Time: In a uni-versal perspective for life on Earth, they are the ulti-mate parents of us all.

From the Rocky Mountains down to the Colorado River, snaking through Grand Canyon in Arizona, water is steadily forming the western landscape. From the frozen ripples and waves and crevasses of the glaciers and snow fields compacting and moving inch by inch, foot by foot, over the years, south to the plunging whitewater rapids dashing over fallen rocks and sweeping through canyon walls in the narrow reaches of the Colorado River, water is ceaselessly re-forming the landscape. And despite the jagged up-thrust of the Canadian Rockies and the gigantic trench of Grand Canyon, there are certain consistencies linking the two. In the glacial flow, the boulders, rock, gravel, and powdered stone pushed along the bottom and the lateral moraines slowly grind away the surface of the host mountain. In the channels of the river, the fallen debris from the collapsing layers of the enclosing canyon walls inexorably widen and deepen the chasm.

Allowing only for the enormous difference in speed and time, the friction of the flow, the processes of wear and attrition are surprisingly similar. Both glacier and river follow the inevitable laws of gravity. They are tortoise and hare in the unequal race down to the level ocean, seeking the channel of least resistance and overcoming that resistance with the power of their weight and movement during the abrasive periods of their flow.

Both glacier and river move relatively fast in the middle, where they encounter the least resistance, while they drag more slowly at the sides, where the friction against solid matter impedes the downward flow. In the process, allowing again only for differential in time, they follow the same process of carving, breaking, and reshaping the ancient in-vestments of the Earth, the geological build-up of layered rock through which the pull of gravity impels them.

The rising and falling shorelines of Great Salt Lake illustrate a basic confusion in our civilized ideas of property measured off by the geometric subdivision of the Earth. Conventional law often fails to deal with natural shifts and alterations in coastal matters. Marine law is equally difficult to apply here. As a result, the changeable intersections, whenever sea meets land, dramatize the clash between dynamic Earth processes and the intransigence of static human conceptual models.

This clash is really a confusion of time (sea) and space (land)— of our sense of the nervous, shifting, volatile movement of the sea against the apparently steadfast permanence of mountains and the solid substance of landforms, as if the interaction between the two were some sort of local argument about jurisdiction in a coastal dispute over ownership and dominion.

The sea provides us our figure in the natural world for time. We speak, metaphorically but accurately, of the "tides of time." Such popular metaphorical expressions also help to define us. When the compulsions of our spatially oriented lives ("A place for everything and everything in its place," "God's in his heaven and all's right with the world," "Keep your house in order") clash with the impulsive variations of temporal change ("Time and tide wait for no man," "If you don't like the weather, wait around for five minutes"), we are said to be, in our confusion, "all at sea."

As a matter of fact, anyone who has been at sea and out of the sight of stabilizing land for any length of time knows how the sense of rigid, measurable space must give way to the fluid rhythms of seatime. Just as we develop "sea legs" to accommodate our own physical movements to those of the ship and the shifting sea, we develop a mental attitude or stance to accommodate, at sea, to the dominance of temporal over spatial orientation.

Years ago, in the age of luxury liners, this led to the common prescription of a long sea voyage to change one's perspective and recover from the disorder and stress of problems in one's land-locked life. Today, it probably helps to account for the popularity of what canny travel agents call "leisure cruises," meaning a sea-going journey with a state of mind and re-creation as its purpose, as its "destination."

We associate sand with the seashore. Fair enough. The attrition of erosion by water made it. But even the most basic knowledge of geology accounts for sedimentary rock, for the compaction of minute grains into sandstone, for limestone, deposited in beds by seas and sufficient time.

The cycles of Earth change make sand the right substance to pass through the narrow eye of the hourglass to measure our small units of time. It measures eons as well. How far-seeing was William Blake's advice to "see eternity in a grain of sand."

A nice journal entry from Capt. Howard Stansbury's 1852 "Exploration and Survey of the Valley of the Great Salt Lake," commenting on the presence of waterfowl in his reconnaissance along the desolate western shoreline:

> Monday, October 22—Morning clear and calm. The Salt Lake, which lay about a half mile to the eastward, was covered by immense flocks of wild geese and ducks, among which many swans were seen, being distinguishable by their size and the whiteness of their plumage. I had seen large flocks of these birds before, in various parts of our country, and especially upon the Potomac, but never did I behold any thing like the immense numbers here congregated together. Thousands of acres, as far as the eye could reach, seemed literally covered with them, presenting a scene of busy, animated cheerfulness, in most graceful contrast with the dreary, silent solitude by which we were immediately surrounded.

It was likely he was looking eastward at Gunnison Island, which still harbors the nesting sites of such fowl, including white pelicans.

I imagine most of us have seen the standard postcard photos from the Great Salt Lake showing bathers floating virtually on top of the water like corks. It is an exhilarating experience. Everyone wants to do it—once. Swimmers are completely frustrated, but bathers take pleasure in it, until they inadvertently get the stinging brine in their eyes or mouth.

The best firsthand account of these sensations of immersion in the waters of the Great Salt Lake is still the earliest. Here is Capt. Howard Stansbury once again:

No one, without witnessing it, can form any idea of the buoyant properties of this singular water. A man may float, stretched at full length, upon his back, having his head and neck, both his legs to the knee, and both arms to the elbow, entirely out of the water. If a sitting position be assumed, with the arms extended to preserve the equilibrium, the shoulders will remain above the surface. The water is nevertheless extremely difficult to swim in, on account of the constant tendency of the lower extremities to rise above it. The brine, too, is so strong that the least particle of it getting into the eyes produces the most acute pain; and if accidentally swallowed, rapid strangulation must ensue. I doubt whether the most expert swimmer could long preserve himself from drowning, if exposed to the action of a rough sea.

Once, Capt. Stansbury recorded, one of his men fell overboard during their exploration of the Lake. Although a good swimmer, he took in some mouthfuls of water before he could be pulled back aboard. "The effect," wrote Stansbury, "was a most violent paroxysm of strangling and vomiting, and the man was unfit for duty for a day or two afterward. He would inevitably have been drowned had he not received immediate assistance."

≈

In a photograph all time is reduced to a single visual image. When we view a geological landscape, the visual image can be expanded to all time.

≈

Of the French Impressionist painters, only Cézanne seems to have had any sense of the underlying geological base of landscape and the life built and being played out upon it. And his concern, like that of all the Impressionists, was with the planes and diversities of light playing on and reflecting from the surfaces. In the bright, nonangular colorations of Auguste Renoir, especially, and best of all, in *The Nymphéas* of Monet, the world is conceivable on canvas only as light, with its variation in color, intensity, and luminous interrelationships. The substratum of the world and its appearances, the dark qualities of hard substances, flat planes, and angles, of rock and landforms divested of botanical growth, is to be found only in some of the scenes of Cézanne. Even these are integrated in compositions of light and dark, being the reflection of light from rock *faces*.

European landscapes across the centuries have reflected age and a sense of the passage of time almost wholly in the guise of the ruins of earlier human civilizations imposed upon forest, meadow, and verdant mountains. No matter how dramatic the scene, no matter how affective the theme of mutability in the inevitable domination of time, the tone of the European landscape is almost always pastoral. Even the up-thrust, jagged, snow-capped peaks of the Alps serve as backdrop to the peacefully domestic alpine valleys below.

The gigantic carved heads of the four presidents on the granite cliffs of Mount Rushmore in the Black Hills of South Dakota embody a strange combination of European and American habits of carving likenesses in stone.

The funerary and effigy sculptures of all the kings and worthies of Europe, including the statues of mythological figures from pre-Christian Greek and Roman anthropomorphism, are free-standing and movable. They are carved *of* stone and are to be found in the cathedrals and crypts and museums throughout Europe. But the Mount Rushmore figures are carved *in* stone, as are those of the partially completed mountain carving of Chief Crazy Horse, also in the Black Hills of South Dakota, and the historical figures carved in Stone

Mountain, Georgia. They have been conceived and sculpted as an integrated part of the natural scene.

In this respect, I think they express that part of the American character which finds and celebrates its identity with the land itself, and especially with the association of stone with permanence and mountains with aspiration. This American carving of human figures into the stone faces of mountains is European in respect to its anthropomorphism. Yet it is probably closer in spirit to the primitivism of prehistoric art, of rock art and cave painting, a means of accommodating the human form to the landscape, of animating the apparently ageless geological face of nature with figures from organic life, memorialized beyond their own biological time. And instead of churches and tombs and cathedrals as the repositories to house these stone representations, these American sculptures are a part of the natural scene itself. The natural settings become the temple within which the generations to come can view them with awe, wonder, and respect, and a kind of worship within the spell of inspiring scenery.

Seen against the slow inevitabilities of geomorphic process, it is instructive to consider the legal fiction of the private ownership of land, or of leases "from the government ownership of land held in the public trust." There is a curious imposition in these matters of ownership of what we've come to think of as "real estate" (which is neither anyone's true *estate*, nor in any but the shortest view of ownership *real*).

I think of the mathematical—that is, abstract or conceptual—sub-division of land by means of the surveyor's measurements, a gridwork laid over the landscape, an artificial, regularized configuration. Actually, it carries down to our own times a left-over pre-Renaissance notion of a flat world. It has become a modern answer to the classic alchemist's problem of squaring the circle, reducing the global Earth to the figures of plane geometry—ideal rather than real, as if there were no such dimension as time.

The Native American view of the landscapes in which they lived helps to make clear the arrogance and mockery explicit in our buying and selling of "real estate."

Land accounts for only two-sevenths of the current surface of the Earth; the rest is salt sea.

The "ownership" of land is a curious expropriation anywhere. It seems particularly inappropriate in the basin and range country of Utah and Nevada, where geological processes have so clearly marked off the land shapes. Any ownership of land, whether private, corporate, state, or federal, is the legal fiction we operate by in the designation and sanctity of property and "real estate."

In the mountain and desert West of America, this fiction sets up an interesting area of conflict with geomorphic time, change, and the ultimate realities of "development." It reduces time from Earth terms to human terms, and loses dimension in the process. It reduces actual landscape, which surrounds us, to the graphic landscape—at worst that of the surveyor's grid-work, and at best the rectangular framework of the photograph or the painter's two-dimensional representation. It ignores in any but legal terms the dimension of time.

Thomas Jefferson knew what he was about when he substituted the American (New World) notion in the Declaration of Independence of a legal guarantee of "life, liberty, and the pursuit of happiness" for John Locke's European (Old World) "life, liberty, and property." The land concept of Locke-ian democracy is basically static, while that of Jefferson is tuned to opportunity and is dynamic.

~

To Henry Thoreau, private "property" was the personal experience attached to the natural setting in which it takes place—as in Walden—rather than exclusive ownership. Actually, the land, or property, he used for his experiment in living at Walden Pond was *owned* by his friend and Concord neighbor Ralph Waldo Emerson.

~

Who owns Great Salt Lake? I don't really know. I wonder, but I don't have much occasion to care. Just looking at it and knowing something of its story, I can suppose maybe I do. Some agency of "the Government," no doubt—or an overlapping combination thereof.

But it is really "owned" by its own history, by the substrate land underneath that it occupies; by its singular, land-locked, self-enclosed place on our maps in the state of Utah. Water flows in from a variety of sources, but none flows out, giving it cause to shift, to rise and fall by itself, thus sealing apart its identity as an inland salt sea. I can't help thinking it owns itself.

~

Individualism, when it is overemphasized, becomes narcissism, which in society is a type of specialization.

~

I see at least two developments in contemporary society that work against specialization: One is the team pattern of approach to complex problems in government and business, science, and technological advance; that is, the recombination of experts. Usually, though, this approach is likened to a short-term assault and reflects that attitude in its language. Military mimicry—"task forces" for this or that—and sports terminology tend to take over.

The other is the return of adults—especially older women whose children have all been raised—to their own delayed higher education.

Since the landscape in which Great Salt Lake is set is similar in so many ways to that of Jerusalem, maybe these Salt Lake Papers have some remote relationship with the Dead Sea Scrolls. There are ways in which the Dead Sea Scrolls themselves are linked to their landscape, to the "Holy Land," which is set in the same kind of semidesert, heavily eroded, mineral landscape, with the Dead Sea, the saltiest in the world, without outlet.

Is there any land which is not "holy land"?

It could be said that this terrain in the Great Basin, with growth and life so sparse, is "wholly land."

The wilderness movement in America is founded in the recognition that the vital sense of privacy at the heart of both American individualism and the sanctity of private property is to be found not where private property lines can be clearly drawn and legally separated, guaranteed, and protected, but rather in the public lands, where the wholeness of the surrounding landscape submerges the individual in it and is not subject to sub-division for any but the broadest common human interest—basically neither economic nor political, but geographical.

Geography

Our concept of geography is devolving rapidly among the professionals in the field but slowly, if at all, in society at large. In conventional older textbook approaches to the subject of geography through the chain of generations living at the end of the twentieth century, the emphasis has been on political ownership, habitation, economic systems, and government. The old globe in schoolrooms was not a planet but a sphere of patchwork colors marking political divisions. At least the color blue showing the oceans gave notice of the dominance of seawater on our aqueous planet. And it was the blue seas that gave shape and distinction to the major landforms, the continents we grew familiar with by names derived from human myth and history: Europe, Asia, Africa, and the Americas, North and South.

But even the enveloping seas that contained them carried similar designations: the vast Atlantic and Pacific Oceans in particular, for they had been the great historical barriers between the peopled lands. These seas, too, were bisected and crisscrossed by the overseas trade routes marked by dotted lines with their given names on the old globe. Equally important to our visual concept of Earth, the oceans and land masses had all been drawn and quartered, so to speak, enmeshed in the geometric net of latitude and longitude lines. All this was visually rather than abstractly imposed on the surface of the globe. It was the earliest and most basic instance of the surveyors' subdivision of Earth.

For centuries, these impositions upon the face of our native planet have dominated the geographical imagery of our world. This was the product of human cartography—mapmaking on a global basis, fragmenting the whole in order to ensure the conceptual autonomy (and thus the contention) of its political parts. This was the *graph* in geography.

The text that followed out this image in language, informing our concepts with facts, figures, and descriptions, left no doubt that geography was not a natural but a social science. It was human history projected upon the setting of the natural world. Any awareness of the organic interrelatedness of that natural world was patently subservient to human life, political differentiation, and destiny. Geography, to put it bluntly, has been the study of human civilization *in situ*. Apparently, to the great majority of nations and peoples on our planet, it still is. Despite the prodigious progress in the natural sciences and technologies, we seem arrested in those self-centered notions that have presided over popular concepts and the uses of geography. How antiquated those old geography books that most of us were led through seem nowadays. Yet how persistently we accept and follow those outdated concepts in our everyday socialized, politicized lives.

We continue as humans to separate history from pre-history, geography from geology and geophysics. I think of the old conventional mode of beginning the study of geography, as many of us were taught in the twentieth century, in Mesopotamia, presumably, though in some respects rather arbitrarily, the cradle of civilization. That is, the cradle of European or "Western" Civilization, it should be added, although we persist in calling that area, now modern Iraq, part of the "Middle East" or the "Muslim World." But that gets us into another means of subdivision and geography according to religious history, and we'd do well to avoid that approach. It could be the most devastating sidetrack of all.

At least the name "Mesopotamia," as we were properly taught, described the nature of that ancient land itself, being the fertile earth, suitable for early agriculture, lying between two rivers, the good old Tigris and Euphrates. I remember what I was taught. But no one ever noted where *those* names came from.

Anyway, the native imagery in those facts from early history featured some balance between those ancient people and the natural history of their Earthly place. That was before the study of Geography (with a capital "G") turned to catalogues of commerce and the individuation of principalities, the economics of commercial development, the exploitation of natural resources, and the geopolitics of modern nationhood.

My interest in what I call geography (with a small "g") began with that scene and continues to this day. But as my schooling progressed, my interest in Geography as a subject dwindled when its stories of the interplay between people and their physical environment became increasingly buried under layers of inert lists citing chief products, both agricultural and industrial; exports and imports; population statistics; comparative wealth and poverty; trade routes and the transportation of goods; major cities; demographics; and so forth. For the continuation of this approach, look at the summary entries for geographical places in any standard encyclopedia—or, I dare say, at least at this point, their equivalent on computer info-networks.

I find new and appropriate suggestion in the lyrics to the favorite old hymn "Rock of Ages" in relation to our developing geological perspectives, within which traditional religious symbolism must adapt:

> Rock of ages, cleft for me,
> Let me hide myself in thee;
> Let the water and the blood,
> From thy riven side which flowed,
> Be of sin the double cure,
> Cleanse me from its guilt and power...

"Carved in stone." From the earliest times of human record—from even the symbolic records of pre-history—in pictographs, petroglyphs, and cave paintings, the most sacred and important matters have been made a part of the apparent permanence of stone. Law, as if its concepts themselves were substantial and for all time, was traditionally writ in stone. The Rosetta Stone and Moses's stone tablets are familiar instances, and the stone stele on which the ancient Code of Hammurabi, the Babylonian lawgiver, was inscribed. The whole matter of *in*scription, for that matter, as against the merely ephemeral *script*. And then came *scripture*.

~~~

Our capacity for variety and ambiguity in respect to both space (dimension) and time (duration) must develop in keeping with the vistas of our knowledge. As astronomy and space travel, together with microscopy and quantum physics, stretch our credulity, we need to shift perspectives from points in time and space to virtual infinity and eternity without stumbling, absorbing contradiction as we do in all matters of dynamic faith.

~~~

Consider the phrase "blind faith." It is applicable in two ways. One signals the way a blind person moves through physical reality, which he has to "see feelingly," to use Gloucester's phrase in *King Lear*, dealing with the unseen by a measure of faith drawn from such sensual data as he *does* have, and moving always with care, heeding all forms of information that help him visualize and proceed on his way.

The other is the tunnel vision of the religious fundamentalist or zealot, following only the straight and narrow without allowing for deviation, oblivious to any features of his world and his conduct in it that are tangential to his own set course—features that come from his "blind" side.

~~~

Here is a potential epigraph for me from John Keats (which rebukes the line of the later poet—was it Auden or was it Eliot?—that "poetry makes nothing happen"):

What benefit canst thou do, or all thy tribe,
To the great world? Thou art a dreaming thing,

A fever of thyself: think of the Earth.

(spoken by the prophetess Moneta in "The Fall of Hyperion")

Art and its religious overtones—what appeals to the spirit and not the marketplace, a sense of personal profit, or the individual artist's aggrandizement—have always had some basic relationship. That is why cave paintings are so mysteriously moving. And our native rock art—the pictographs and petroglyphs of the Southwest—as well, wedding art to nature and spirit integrated with the ecosystems of landscape.

In his ingenious study *The Origin of Consciousness in the Breakdown of the Bicameral Mind*, Julian Jaynes suggests that the early nineteenth-century discoveries of the geological layering of the Earth led to analogues in human consciousness. By 1875, he says, psychological models also supposed the presence of consciousness was but a surface above multilayered depths of mental life in which the unconscious ruled. Sigmund Freud's model of the psyche draws upon this same analogue.

The record of the Earth's past lies in its geological formations, active, but mostly buried; but here in Utah so much is, almost embarrassingly, exposed. Think of the metaphors of the "buried life," the "buried past," and matters "buried in the past."

Julian Jaynes writing on time concepts: "You cannot, absolutely cannot think of time except by spatializing it. Consciousness is always a spatialization in which the diachronic is turned into the synchronic, in which what has happened in time is excerpted and seen in side-by-sideness." Right on!

My own geological layering, here and there in my "road cuts" and surface erosion, brought about by time and exposed to the passerby…my own epochs and eras…my tree rings as I age….

It was easy right after the rampaging runoff of spring 1983 in the Wasatch Range—with the flooding and debris flushed from the mountains down into the valleys, the gigantic mudslides on the slopes over Farmington, just east of the Great Salt Lake, the acres of silt and tumbling rocks streaming down the sandbag channel through downtown Salt Lake City, thrown up hastily to carry the gigantic overflow of normally tame City Creek off to the Jordan River and thence to Great Salt Lake—to mock the unctuous locution of the Mormons in their weekly broadcast of the Mormon Tabernacle Choir: "From the crossroads of the West in the shadow of the everlasting hills."

The rise of the NOW generations follows from the introduction and mass media spread of photographed "reality." The emphasis on the present instant is imposed by the photographed moment—re- and re- and re-produce-able, unchanged. "Motion" pictures no exception, except psychologically.

In print, no matter how much "immediacy" it suggests, there is a firm background sense for the reader of a split in time between the author's account—that is, the time of writing, of "utterance"— and the NOW of the reader's re-creation in the act and sense of his own moment. With this situation, the emphasis falls chiefly on the re-creation: the reader is the one who is real, who animates, gives life to what he reads. With the photograph, including the sequenced motion picture, the reverse is generally the case. The viewer surrenders reality to it, and *its* time becomes primary and presides over the experience.

~

Ben DeMott quoting Emerson in his Humanities address at Snowbird: "We animate what we can, and we see only what we animate."

~

Grains of sand are forever being recycled—broken and worn down from the rock base, transported and further eroded by wind and water, and collected into beach and dune. Then, by a change of Earth processes in their location, they again become compacted and buried, turning again, in time, to stone.

~

Consider the Biblical sense of our own recycling: "In the sweat of thy face shalt thou eat bread, till thou return unto the ground; for out of it wast thou taken: for dust thou art, and unto dust shalt thou return."—Genesis 3:19

~

Among the Biblical (Old Testament) precedents and references for modern Utah is the naming of Moab, the town closest to Arches and Canyonlands National Parks. Moab, the father of the Moabites "unto this day," was the son of the elder of the two daughters of Lot, who, after accompanying him in flight from Sodom and Gomorrah before those cities of wickedness were destroyed, both got their father drunk on successive nights and lay with him in order to preserve the seed of their father. Thus, the incestuous offspring of Lot, whose poor wife, it will be remembered, looked back as the family fled from the "rain of brimstone and fire" on the ill-fated cities and became a pillar of salt.—Genesis 19:24–38

The Tax in Taxonomy

Humans could be distinguished from the other creatures of Earth as the only list-making animal. According to the account in Genesis, Adam got this under way by naming the rest of the animals. Unfortunately, no one told him that he was one of the lot. Typically, it seems he did not name himself. Or Eve. For they were supposedly given dominion over all the beasts of the field, the fish in the sea, and the birds in the air. That's because, having named them, he had them on his list. It couldn't work the other way around.

Later, long after Adam, we humans all became heirs of Carl Linnaeus, that most compulsive list maker of them all. He might be considered the second Adam in our lineage, the classifier of Earth's biota, systematically locating all living forms known to his mid-eighteenth-century world in a stable list with their Latin names. Stable, for Latin was a dead language, written but no longer evolving in speech. Since then, we all persist in the human mania for naming. If we pretend to be scientific about it, we call our naming *taxonomy*.

I'm no exception. I want to know the names of things. I want to distinguish the red pines from the white pines, the cedar from the spruce and the fir. I want to know the names of all the wildflowers I see and to that extent, I guess, to tame them. If I'm really into it, I can list those I haven't seen as well. Knowing them by name gives me that right, gives me that power. For it is the power in the naming that we want.

Now and then, usually suddenly, I become aware of the vanity in this human habit, this compulsive behavior of my species. One of those naming and listing situations will suddenly point up the anthropomorphism involved. Such as the naming and classifying of our pets, although I suppose their willing dependency on us, being tame and domesticated, helps to justify that practice.

When we're in the wild, our way of appropriating things in their native places—that is, when they are in their natural setting and we are transients—is to assume a proprietary relationship. We combine our acquisitive nature with our need to attach names to everything.

It can happen here, let's say, at a desert creek-side campsite. The garter snake that inhabits the grassy base of a rocky ledge near my tent and makes his slithery rounds every morning becomes "my" snake. If I'm really civilized about it—Disneyfied, we might say in these latter days when the world according to Walt has found a way to tame everything that was once wild and thus nameless—I might even call it Sammy Snake or Sarah Snake, depending on which gender I wish it to represent on my list of local flora and fauna. The jack pine (there's a name) where I hang my canteen becomes "my canteen tree" and thus is robbed in my mind of its own wild existence, which is to say its own vital integrity.

There, finally, lies the paradox in this naming business. For to bestow a name on anything alive on our planet robs it in our minds of its distinction, its oneness on Earth. Classification, that human rage for order, is at once the means of acknowledging distinctions in the world around us and of denying the life force independently present in each segment of our incredibly rich, ancient, and diversified biosphere.

This is the root problem in our current dilemma about the natural world and the "management of wilderness." It is the human need to name, to designate, and to classify, which now brings us, to use Bill McKibben's phrase, to the end of nature, at least as we have assumed and thus appropriated *that* name up to now.

If I take it full circle back to the Old Testament naming of Adam and Eve, it is the old business of eating the fruit of the tree of knowledge, the fall of the primal innocence of Eden, which is to say, the state of nature before notions of corruption or evil entered with our species.

If you ask me, Adam's problem—and ours in consequence—began when he named the tree "tree" and proceeded to classify it as

"fruit tree" and then to specify it as "apple." Just eating of it would
have been natural enough and okay. If he'd just known he was an animal. But no, he had to go and name it. That made it forever *his* apple.
I wish it had really become stuck in his throat. Instead, on down the
line, for better or for worse, alas, it has become ours as well.

≈

When the strong winds preceding a weather front from the west or
northwest cross the salt flats, they pick up the light specks, the salt
sands, of the flats. Carried to the city over the Great Salt Lake, these
dissolve in the moisture of the gathering storm and are spattered on
the west side of houses with the raindrops. Thus one of the hazards
of painting your house dark colors in Salt Lake City (or the Wasatch
Front) is the irregular gray-white coating such salt storms leave on your
siding when it dries out.

≈

It is easy in the blush of our technological success with electronics
to miss the significance of the fact that we now commit the memory of our species to a mineral repository—that is, to the silicon chips
on which we etch the circuits of our accumulated conceptions and
knowledge. The analogy to the Earth's past, the planet's memory, you
could say, is being recorded and held in the mineral strata of geomorphic time. The result is striking, to say the least. The silicon chips reflect our lives in microcosm; the geological forms of the Earth show
us our larger selves in macrocosmic detail.

(Perhaps pre-digitalized photography, with its dependence on
chemicals and the sensitivity of silver nitrate to light, falls in the same
category of this reflection.)

≈

There are two slightly different ways that people pronounce *Utah*,
one of which was exploited by the State Travel Agency or Tourist

Bureau in its promotion materials by typographical spelling of the state's name as an exclamation of pleasure: *UtAH!* The second pronunciation, with a lowering of the second vowel, has yet to be exploited in a similar way but is just as likely a prospect for interesting expression of the state's attributes—especially those marvels of geomorphology revealed in the landforms of the state: *UtAWE.*

Tectonics and the hydrothermal activity in the great fissures of ocean bottoms are perpetually altering the chemical composition of the world's seawater and its salinity. The Great Salt Lake, on the other hand, is in effect a huge passive bowl (or platter) into which rivers with their sources in mountains' drainages discharge their mineral-laden flow. The Lake, being subject to a high rate of evaporation in its normally dry climate, acts as a large evaporation pan for an enormous expanse of surface area. The chemistry of the Lake, unlike the oceans, is altered more according to surface activities rather than subsurface forces and materials.

For the last fifty years or so, the level of the Dead Sea has been falling. Like Great Salt Lake, tectonics formed its basin, which is a continuation of the African rift system known sometimes as the Dead Sea Rift. Runoff is evidently less in the area surrounding the Dead Sea than it is in Utah around Great Salt Lake, and the heat/evaporation process is greater, although there are abundant hot springs along the western shore. In addition, the Israelis have diverted the Jordan River for water to serve the growing population and threaten thereby to further use up the Lake's tributaries, thus cutting down or off the main supply of new water to the repository of the Dead Sea.

The Great Smoky Mountains, part of the Appalachian chain, are some of the oldest mountains in the world, although they exist on the same continent as the relatively young Rockies. The Smokies are quite worn and rounded by erosion and are thickly forested, although they may originally have stood as tall as the Asian Himalayas do today.

Flooding from the heavy spring runoff shows me dramatically, and virtually in my own backyard, the erosive force of descending water—in this instance in familiar Mill Creek, where I have hiked and loafed and meditated for twenty years while the water trickled and gurgled peaceably within its meandering stream bed. Now it has dashed and chewed its way into the earth in what are actually the beginnings of small canyons, displacing and carrying off great chunks of soil and rock and vegetation to effect an alarming transformation.

The major changes have been vertical rather than horizontal, which is what the easterner or midwesterner expects of flooding in the open flood plains of his rivers. First the cut down through earth and loosened rock, then the horizontal—the mud and rock spread over the few flat meadow areas where silt, rock, and debris from the normally passive creek spread out and cover all the normal green growth.

7/30/83 Church Fork, Mill Creek Canyon

John McPhee's phrase (is it HIS?) for the "flow" of earthscape (my own term—but is it mine?) to be seen and felt as it is caught and molded in geological formations: "rivers in rock," he calls it.

The Colorado River falls two miles over its "exotic" 1,400-mile course. This is largely a matter of the land it drains—the Colorado

Plateau, having risen by geomorphic forces eons earlier, giving its drainage the power to fall and become increasingly abrasive in its passage to the sea. The Mississippi, I read somewhere, flows 2,550 miles, falls only one-third of a mile over its length. (I'd better check this…)

If cave paintings and the pre-historic petroglyphs and pictographs of the American mountain and desert Southwest are a valid indication, what humans have worshipped in one form or another throughout the ages (both historical and pre-historical) is their own imagination. In modern times we have been inclined to think we have worshipped the *products* of our imagination, as if we were not somehow involved with and responsible for them—as if we, in our imaginative moments, were not the key and controlling factor.

But it is still our imagination itself that deserves and gets our faith, whether we call the form it takes science or technology or poetry or religion. It is human imagination, the formulating cause—to use one of Aristotle's four causes—that controls the power we have to alter the world according to design and purpose, for good or ill, to ameliorate, to purposefully maintain, to create, and to destroy. The efficient modeling in the imagination precedes the efficient action performed in the physical world.

Where seismic activity occurs every one thousand years or so, this, to geologists, is regarded as *continuous activity.*

Plate tectonics came into clear focus in the 1960s as the result of extensive monitoring through seismographs of the Earth's patterns of earthquakes. Ironically, this came about from the proliferation of nuclear bomb testing around the globe during the years of "hippie" revolt.

The roots of the term "geology" from the ancient Greek:
geo: earth
logy: discourse

Biblical passages having to do with geography in the Holy Land which are, fortuitously, applicable to Utah and the Great Basin, and thus available to the Mormons' modern Zion:

> The voice of him that crieth in the wilderness, Prepare ye the way of the Lord, make straight in the desert a highway for our God.
> Every valley shall be exalted (lifted up), and every mountain and hill shall be made low: and the crooked shall be made straight, and the rough places plain (the uneven ground shall become level and the rough places a plain).
>
> —from Isaiah 40:3–4 (quoted in Luke 3:5)

Chronological periods of Earth time are separated and identified in increasingly specific terms by geologists, breaking it into more and more discrete segments. Yet time itself is continuous and has in its own inexorable movement no regular time divisions. Geological layering and geological time periods or eras are, like clocks, mechanical measurements superimposed on continuous time in order to measure it and isolate events. Unlike time itself, they are linked to visual records of changes in time, again like clocks.

This has been accentuated in our clock-time nowadays, by clocks that jump from minute to minute rather than sweeping uninterrupted through the circular face of minutes, hours, and days; then by the vogue of digital clocks, which deal even more mysteriously in visual numbers in sequence, with no indication of the passage of time between.

According to E.V. Rawley of the Utah Dept. of Natural Resources, Division of Wildlife Resources, "The marshes of the Great Salt Lake are probably the most important single breeding ground for waterfowl that now remains in the United States." He says, "These marshes are essential to the preservation of international populations of migratory waterfowl, and in maintaining the distribution of these birds."

Carp, which are found in abundance in most drainages that empty into Great Salt Lake, are native to Asia. They were introduced into Utah in 1881—the same carp that now infest the muddy waters of the Colorado and that I have heard night after night flopping in the easy waters of the lower Grand Canyon. I also remember them doing their lazy flopovers on the surface of the streams that channel into the Bear River Bird Refuge. They were like something quite ancient and antediluvian, with their scales like armor plate that you almost expected to clank as they curved and maneuvered sluggishly in the roiling water. The only comparable fish in my experience is the bottom-feeding tarpon I caught once with my cousin, Len DeMichele, in the Gulf of Mexico bays of the west coast of Florida off Boca Grande.

The islands in Great Salt Lake are important rookeries for a number of species besides the California gulls that are historically linked, thanks to their gluttony, to the struggles of the Mormon pioneers beset by hordes of crickets. Records show that all the islands, protecting against predators, hosted nesting colonies in the past, including great blue herons and double-crested cormorants. Now some of the islands still serve—most notably for the gulls and, on Gunnison Island, for the white pelicans.

Antelope Island was named by John C. Fremont, who undertook the first "scientific" examination of the Lake in 1843 by paddling what his account calls his "India rubber boat" with four companions from the mouth of the Weber River out to the island now known as "Fremont Island" (named by Stansbury). Back again in 1845, Fremont and his men conducted a successful antelope hunt on horseback between the mainland on the east and the island (at that time clearly a peninsula, which, with the recent rise of the Lake level, it no longer is). They referred to it as Antelope Island, and the name stuck—although in early Mormon days it was commonly called Church Island locally, and by some people in the vicinity still is. Nowadays there is an introduced buffalo herd maintained there.

Saltair, the most famous and elaborate of the Great Salt Lake resorts, was completed in 1893. It was a huge pavilion with bathing houses and facilities around it and a central dance hall under the onion-shaped turrets that suggested oriental splendor within. Originally built on pilings out into the Lake in five feet of water, it survived the variations in water levels until the exceptionally low levels of the 1960s left it high and dry. Business fell off and the resort was literally abandoned. A series of small fires and vandalism reduced it to a shell, still imposing and full of ghosts when I first saw it in the late '60s. Nobody else around. Our kids felt the romance of the abandoned glory in their own peculiar ways.

I recall clearly watching the plumes of black smoke that took it in the final fire of 1970. We watched from our deck at home, looking out over the city, over the bustling airport to the shores of Great Salt Lake. It burned and smoldered for days. Later, all the remaining debris was cleared away, and there is nothing left at that spot to show for the opulent resort the natives called "the Lady of the Lake."

There are isolated populations of mammal species that hibernate in the winter throughout the Great Basin, isolated with the disappearance of Lake Bonneville to the surrounding areas of springs and marshes. The pocket gopher sub-species are a model of this and have been much studied.

Great Salt Lake is normally about six times saltier than the oceans.

Captain Stansbury—for whom the Stansbury Mountain Range and its continuation as a semi-island ridge in the Great Salt Lake, which is called Stansbury Island, are named—began his extensive exploration of the Lake in 1849, two years after the first Mormon pioneers arrived. He was probably the first white man to circle the Lake on land. The next year he and his crew made a complete survey of the Lake. He also sounded the Lake for the first time.

In 1869–70, the Fortieth Parallel Survey made another complete survey of the Lake. At this time, twenty years after the Stansbury survey, the Lake was considerably higher. The contrast of their map with that of Stansbury is interesting and instructive. The shape of the Lake is hardly a constant, and wasn't the same a century ago and more.

At one point, midway in the accumulation of these notes and items, I decided that I should circumnavigate Great Salt Lake for myself. I had no trouble enlisting my colleague Ken Eble to accompany me in my four-wheel-drive Toyota. I needed to authenticate my coverage by seeing it, personally, as a whole, from a circuit of the full perimeter of that strange, huge inland sea with no outlet and water many times saltier than the oceans. I wanted to feel the whole of its mystique and stark beauty—so much water set in that high-desert landscape with virtually no growth or green on its barren shores to mask it.

All civilized approaches are from either the south or the populated eastern side, notably via the long causeway built to take tourists and natives alike out to Antelope Island. Less accessible is the irregular north shore, although there are some vagrant dirt roads there.

One runs south, roughly from the isolated Golden Spike Historical Monument (where the transcontinental railroad lines were joined, an event celebrated and re-enacted annually). If you stay with this, it can take you to a deserted shoreline where *Spiral Jetty*, Robert Smithson's 1970 earthworks sculpture, can still be seen, either above or below the shallow water as the Lake levels vary.

From that point on, though, staying always near or at least in sight of the Lake as we continued our counterclockwise circumnavigation, Ken and I found no dirt roads, and only intermittent, half-visible car tracks to follow. This was in the late 1970s or early '80s. There was little reason for anyone to be in that wasteland, unless they were such curious—and heedless—venturers as we. I doubt that much has changed there in the years since.

It was slow going, but we had time to be leisurely, pausing often to get out and survey our scene. For two nights, we stopped early to explore a likely area, eat a simple camper's supper, and relax. As was our custom, we talked unguardedly wherever our thoughts took us. Finally, we settled on the open ground, nestled in our sleeping bags under an incredibly clear, star-filled desert night sky, happy with the day's adventure, silent and contemplative before deep sleep—until daybreak.

Well, I have to qualify that. We didn't sleep through the second night. At some indeterminate time that night, the air and our sleep were torn open and shattered by a tremendous roar suddenly and immediately over our heads. We were stunned awake as, just as suddenly, the explosive roar was over and gone. A pair of jet fighter planes on a low altitude night run from Hill Air Force Base across the Lake had buzzed us. We were either illegally on or dangerously near their designated bombing range.

We knew of the bombing range from studying maps before our trip. But the restricted area stretched for a hundred miles west over the empty salt desert, practically to the Nevada border. We had blithely—let's admit it, stupidly—supposed that didn't apply to the Great Salt Lake. If we stayed along the shoreline we would not be interlopers on forbidden territory.

I should say "I," since the idea of the trip was mine, as were the preparations. I expected the trip would help personalize and authenticate my notes. Ken was, sort of, along for the ride. I probably thought, vainly if at all, that as university professors conducting some kind of professional research we could assume immunity. Innocent arrogance or just plain stupid? Well, something of both.

We didn't talk much about the jet fighters the next morning, but just shook our heads and went about our business of getting under way. That is, until we were shortly confronted by the government sign clearly marking the restricted area ahead, with no-nonsense notice about danger and punishment for unauthorized trespass. Nothing was said about exemptions for professors on a casual lark. I have a vague recollection of Ken saying softly, "Ohhh shhit." We stared at each other for a spell before I turned the car around and headed back the way we'd come.

One hardly ever sees the mammals of the Great Basin and the areas surrounding the Great Salt Lake except two large ones, the mule deer and the pronghorns. Elk and moose do not get out in the Great Basin itself, only coming down to the fringe mountain level. Yet there are over a hundred species of mammals in the region identified in the immediate environment of Great Salt Lake itself, the so-called Homo sapiens being but one. Sizes vary all the way from the three-gram ring-tailed shrew to moose that weigh up to four hundred kilograms.

The smaller mammals are in many ways the most interesting. One kangaroo rat can live entirely on the moisture metabolized by its own kidneys. In the mountain ranges, voles populate the meadows. They are relatives of muskrats and lemmings, and usually produce five litters per year. Occasionally, for a cluster of reasons biologists of the area have not yet identified, the voles have population surges. In 1957–58, there was such an explosion of voles, in numbers estimated at some choice vole habitats at three thousand per acre.

Ground squirrels vary their litters from one to sixteen, an extraordinarily large variation that is demonstrably related to the quantity and quality of precipitation of the period during and immediately following gestation, which takes place within thirty days of their emergence in February.

Pack rats, who really do collect strange items to line their nests, are related closely to the big-eared deer mice. The Great Basin has some six kinds of deer mice and about twenty species of bats.

Somewhat larger, but seen just as rarely, is the kit fox. He is a true desert fox, expert in catching the elusive kangaroo rats. Kit foxes curiously do not show any special fear of man, probably because they see few and have never been hunted for their fur.

The badger, a member of the weasel family, specializes in Great Basin ground squirrels, being able to dig them out of their burrows when they're in hibernation.

⁓

Dinosaurs dominated the Earth for 130 million years. What we now call Utah has more than its share of their ossified remains.

⁓

Reptiles get their body heat directly from sunlight and cannot produce it or regulate it from within. We humans use about 80% of our food for producing and regulating our body heat, keeping it normally at 98.6 degrees F. Reptiles use only about 10% for regulating the heat they absorb directly from the sun. Thus they are adapted to their desert existence.

~

The Navajo considers the landscape he lives in and moves through not just as surrounding countryside or scenery. It also lies within. Its configurations and processes are an intimate extension of his personhood. His personhood is an intimate extension and feature of the landscape.

~

As you develop a geological sense of the landscape around Salt Lake City, what is revealed of the past levels of ancient waters in the east, and south hill-side "benches" left from Lake Bonneville, actually become *benchmarks* of the place.

~

The Dominguez-Escalante party entered Utah in 1776, made it from Colorado as far as Utah Valley to the south, heard of a great salt lake to the north, but with winter threatening, turned south and never saw it.

~

"The Wasatch line," says Lee Stokes, is "the most profound geological discontinuity on the North American continent."

~

Salt Lake City has been on a shoreline twenty-three times throughout the various geological periods. (Lee Stokes lecture)

At an average depth of a mere thirteen feet, Great Salt Lake is nothing to the geological substratum depths below it.

Geology is named for Gaea, who was the daughter of Chaos—that is, she personifies Earth, having sprung from primeval CHAOS. Gaea in turn bore from herself, unaided, Ouranos, the Sky. Then, mating with him, she bore the first Titans, the Cyclopes, and the Hekatoncheires, or hundred-handed giants.

The Great Basin has gone through a number of our planet's ice ages. The most recent glacial epoch took place from about thirty-three thousand to thirteen thousand years ago. There are still old glacial erratics on the tops of some Great Basin mountains, deposited there when the most recent glaciers melted their last. The glaciation previous to this one in the Great Basin area was seven hundred million years ago.

Lake Bonneville's shoreline was at its highest level fourteen thousand to sixteen thousand years ago. Then, thirteen thousand to fourteen thousand years ago, Lake Bonneville spilled over and cut through an outlet north of the Cache Valley, in what has become the Snake River in Idaho. The outlet was in Idaho just above Red Rock Pass. Enormous amounts of water escaped in a very short time.

The salt and minerals have been collecting in the Great Salt Lake ever since Lake Bonneville quit overflowing through Red Rock Pass, Idaho, some thirteen thousand years ago. The Lake probably reached something close to its current level with the disappearance of the most recent ice age, a period confirmed by evidence from deep sea sources as well as from geomorphic surface evidence. The level of Great Salt Lake has thus fluctuated at about its current level for well over ten thousand years.

～

The historic low of Great Salt Lake was reached about 1963 at 4,191.6 feet. The highest recorded depth was set in 1873 at 4,211.5 feet. Set against the thirteen thousand years since the overflow of Lake Bonneville established the enclosed body of Great Salt Lake, how pitifully small that ninety-year span becomes.

～

Great Salt Lake has two prominent ridges running north and south with a valley in between. The east ridge follows the line of Antelope Island, and Fremont Island to Promontory Point. The west ridge proceeds northward from Stansbury Island. The flocks of white pelicans that nest on Gunnison Island near the top of the west ridge fly some forty to fifty miles to the freshwater inlets on the east and northeast sides of the Lake to feed on fish.

～

Typically, the Eastern approach to life has been based on a pervading sense of its *transience*. The approach of Western Civilization depends on a sense of *change*. The one is a static interlude between enduring states, the other a series of transitions between progressive stages. Maintenance, as Eric Hoffer, the once popular social critic, has pointed out, is important to the West, not to the East.

～

Character is determined by what one respects.

～

Gene Foushee, a retired geologist in Bluff, Utah, uses the word "digestion" for the chemical action that gradually dissolves rock.

Lichen is a symbiotic growth of algae and fungus that attaches itself to rock surfaces and very slowly grows, breaking down that part of the rock's surface in the process.

The phrase "think big" has its origin in American enterprise and capitalist entrepreneurship—how to make a million. It now seems more applicable to concepts of time and space. The problem becomes how to "think big" enough to comprehend the millions of units—years in geological terms, light years in astronomy—that we must now accept as the extent of our own being, our own "moment."

That old hand-game of paper/rock/scissors came to mind today—the circular competition of the two symbols thrown by the players' hands—paper covers rock, rock breaks scissors, scissors cuts paper. A new perspective seems called for in which water and perhaps lichen get involved: water cuts rock, lichen dissolves rock.

Photography must be taken as a form of art. Otherwise it has to be taken as a form of reality. Art involves a transformation, treatment, or reflection of reality.

The photograph and the living, sentient experience are like the two poles of ancient Greek thought: Being and Change.

When strong winds blow, the salt-laden water of Great Salt Lake is so heavy with its specific gravity that it literally blows to the other side or end of the Lake. A north wind, especially, is capable of sweeping over the length of the Lake and shifting so much of the water to the south end that the shoreline at the north will recede greatly.

≈

The spectacle of the Northern Lights playing over the Great Salt Lake presents phenomena well worth observation and speculation— the mineral content of the water in relation to the charged particles, probably of solar origin, glowing in the Earth's magnetic field.

≈

Genevieve Atwood reminds me that the water at the bottom of Great Salt Lake has a greater salinity than that at the surface. It figures. At what depth, I wonder, do the geologists and hydrologists determine and establish the figure for the Lake's salinity?

≈

The Bear River, the Weber River, and the Jordan River systems are the major sources of surface inflow, bringing in approximately 90% of the water and 60% to 80% of the dissolved solids, the rest coming from small streams and canals. But this is just the surface inflow. The Lake is also fed by subsurface or groundwater inflow, although the amount is quite minimal in volume and in the percentage of dissolved solids. Dependable estimates are difficult to obtain. The third source is precipitation—rain and snow. The distribution of this is curious, thanks to the varying landforms and meteorological elements involved.

    The more arid region west of the Lake—over the salt flats to Nevada—with its annual precipitation of 4.5 inches, contributes less to the west side of the Lake than does the temperate, semiarid east side of the Lake (which rises eventually up to the 11,000-foot peaks of the

Wasatch Front), with its average annual precipitation of 16 inches. The best estimates of what percentage of Great Salt Lake's water comes in the form of precipitation run from 25 to 30 percent.

The salinity of the south and east portions of the Lake are generally less than that of the west and north. The reason is the inflow sources entering from the east and south—particularly the Bear, Weber, and Jordan Rivers—and also the higher precipitation figures on the eastern portions than on the western, together with the higher evaporation rate on the dry salt-flat west than the Wasatch Front east.

Before 1959, when the Southern Pacific Railroad built its rock-fill causeway to replace the old wooden trestle crossing that had spanned the Great Salt Lake since its construction in 1902, the Lake was pretty much uniform in its salinity—a continuous, relatively homogenous salt lake. Now the causeway has divided the Lake into essentially two bodies of water: the north arm and the south arm.

The two are surprisingly different in color, clarity, density, and surface level. The brine in the north arm gives it a reddish-pink cast, owing to dominance of the red algae among the few species of algae and bacteria that can survive there. In the somewhat less saline south arm, the blue-green algae prevail, and the color of the water follows suit—much more attractive to the eyes of most viewers. The clarity of the water, or what the hydrologists call "turbidity," varies not only from the north to the south but also from season to season with the changes in algae and inflow patterns. The difference in the density of the north arm and the south arm (that is, the measure of the ion concentrations in the composition of the Lake brine) was always notable, but it has increased since the construction of the SPRR rock causeway, which allows an interchange or equalizing brine transfer through two relatively

small concrete box culverts in the twelve miles of rock fill that girdles
the Lake from east to west.

The unpleasant, fetid smell that often characterizes the shores of
Great Salt Lake varies with the waxing and waning of its causes, all
related in one way or another to the salinity and what it breeds. But
residents anywhere near the shore can be thankful that most of the
potential odor is contained below the surface—particularly in the
south end, where tests at various depths have shown a distinct strat-
ification of the Lake brine and sediments. The deeper the layer, the
more fetid and discolored the brine, until at the lowest layers just
above the sedimentary bottom, the concentrations and detrital materials are at their most noxious. On the open surface, however, there is
only clear, odor-free brine.

We can speak of "child time" and "adult time," the former having a
subjective sense of continuity as its basic mode, the latter having an
objective, unchanging, mathematically divisible mode of measure-
ment—a regulatory parade of instants in lock-step (or clock-step)—
as its basic mode: set by metrics.

On land, child time is more and more difficult to maintain, since
civilization and technology and society depend on the commonly
held, objectively measured "adult" time.

At sea, however, the analogues with divisible units of geographical
space and distance are difficult to apply. The sea is continuous much
as time is to a child, and one naturally adapts one's sense of time and
movement to that same childlike outlook.

My writing—or all formal *literature*, for that matter—is most successful if it has layers and levels of participation, involvement, and

significance for all readers. I should add that it is necessary only for each reader to enter at the level of interest he finds reflective of his own concerns and that perhaps he senses in the levels of metaphor involved beyond these.

In this assertion, I am following the historical lead of the Christian church, which for centuries has carried its aspirations and its apperceptions of truth in ritual ceremonies and liturgies that permit—indeed, decree—that all participate and accept, whether just at the most rote, literal level or with the accumulation of the many layers of symbolic insight, realized or potentially realizable (i.e., through hope and faith), available in the reach of the religious narrative and metaphor celebrated in ritual.

(February 1982, in France)

Our sense of individual identity is both our blessing and our curse. Cemeteries, gravestones, and the wish for individual immortality are symptoms of the curse, of the post-adolescent sense of our mortal lease on life as single human beings. These are attempts to cling to the isolated state of the single desire-centered self.

Of eventual importance, however, as our perspective matures, is the need to escape from the restricting singleness of human existence, to set aside and transcend our individuality, finally, to blend. But it takes a strong individual apperception of relationships—what has usually been manifested as the religious sentiment—to accomplish this sense of belonging to time out of mind as well as belonging to, and filling, the space of our physical, sentient individual lives.

(February 1982, in France)

I must explore the iconography that can carry the symbolic burden of the religious sentiment after the proposed Second Coming—that is, after Christ has come and gone again, this time joining with Mother

Earth rather than with "the Heavenly Father." The need for a meta-phorical base is preeminently the human need and must be served.

Somehow this may be tied in with the nature of and our fealty to the world according to the Photograph—the new ideogram, hiero-glyph, and iconography, picture-writing (relate to the difference be-tween the tourists' snapshots of the West and the art of an Ansel Adams—relate this to the petroglyphs and pictographs of the South-west, the cave paintings I've now seen and marveled at in France and Spain).

Best not to cut off religion in the West from its history—our his-tory—but to view its evolution and continuance into new stages, new dispensations, new levels, new symbolic centers.

I think suddenly, and curiously, of the two meanings, for example, of *scope*. And the Old English *scōp*. (And the irony of the "Scopes" trial of the 1920s.)

(At St. Jean d'Arc, Versailles, during the service, 2-7-82)

Sequence seen from a train in France: a swollen river, just short of flood stage; then sets of rectangular garden plots, drained, planted, and maintained; then a cemetery with the graves and headstones crowded in ranks, shoulder to shoulder, foot to head—each in *its* individual plot; and at the end of the cemetery, the uninterrupted carpet of grass and the regular rows of plain crosses of the military graves, the undifferentiated sites of soldiers "dead in the service of their country."

Four kinds of constructions built on the presiding hilltops and emi-nences of European towns and locales: castles, churches, water tow-ers, and (now) electronic telecommunication relay reflectors.

Vincent Van Gogh, writing about the monumental self-portrait done in Paris in early 1888, the painter in front of his easel: "One seeks after a deeper resemblance than the photographer's." And then I see a viewer in the museum taking a photograph of the painting!

<hr />

ON HISTORY: Past, Present, and Future

A knowledge of history is essential to an active sense of the future and a sensible use of the present. As one opens the past through that knowledge, there is a compensating extension of the historical sense into the future. To the extent that one knows the past, one is thus enabled to project the future. The present then becomes the axis or balancing point, the fulcrum, between them.

Mature points of view—including such "wisdom" as age bestows simply through the accumulation of experience—are examples of these same axioms on a purely personal, individual, experiential basis.

The child's view of the future, as well as his sense of consequence, is directly proportionate to the amount of knowledge, almost entirely through personal experience, he can draw on from the past. The child's sense of future "history" thus is obviously short, and he is typically shortsighted and destructive and self-centered.

The same proportions normally apply throughout a personal life. The active sense of the future normally extends in proportion to the passive knowledge from the past. The peculiar extension of this for socially based humans comes through formal education in the common past—vicarious experience, or knowledge, from what can be established and conveyed of the historical and evolutionary past.

The corollary of this for the sense we need of future history is that we must make this historical and evolutionary knowledge of the past vital in personal terms, so that it becomes an extension both backward and forward of our personal lives, commitments, and identities.

Religious education thus far has been, for better or for worse, a short-circuiting of the historical process in the developing mind of man.

Historical perspective, which conventionally has been simply a practical, pragmatic matter of the bearing of past human experience on our sense of the present, has tended to become religious perspective. Beyond common rational thought, religion proposes *a-historical* grounds for human prophecy, purpose, and determination.

But historical perspective cannot be a matter of religion per se (at least as we have known religion by way of theology and religious history) because religions have always been characterized by superstition and dogma. Historical perspective in this view is precisely the opposite; it should be an escape from dogma. Since history, so conceived, is both factual and prophetic, it serves both the empirical and imaginative needs of human hope. It serves the needs and highest purposes of the religious sentiments without falling back into the cant of organized religions or special, selective revelation. It equates each human life with all human life, but goes beyond the more utilitarian forms of humanism by reaching for Earth's histories and eventualities beyond the mere record of humankind as well.

Thus archaeology, history, biology, and astronomy (or cosmology) are all linked and inseparable except for their differing investigatory data and processes. In this latter sense, they are sciences. But unless they are related in this larger "religious" view of the extension of personal identity, they are, like children, full of potential but shallow in their knowledge of history and, in consequence, self-indulgent, shortsighted, and likely to be destructive.

Any valid representation of "the real world" is necessarily a combination of what we have come to know it to be and what we are able to imagine it may yet be. Which of these is the way of history and which the way of science is an interesting question. In any event, the two functioning together form the matrix, or the metaphor, of human reality.

I remember the Salt Lake Valley in 1944, when I was a World War II serviceman at Kearns Overseas Replacement Depot, at the foot of the Oquirrhs, as smothered by coal smoke in late November through December. I couldn't even see the Wasatch Range across the valley so thick was the pall of coal smoke between.

"Grass roots" is an eastern and midwestern agrarian concept that hardly fits in a geological, rock-face, mountain-desert environment. "Grass-roots movement" in Utah or Nevada is not a very effective figure of speech.

The concern for *ends* is the business and purpose of the Humanities. That is, the judgment of proper ends or goals is best informed by reference to historical perspective, philosophical analysis, and the disciplined imagination, which is given range and vicarious perception through experience in the creative arts. Science and technology are never more than the *means* to achieve the desirable ends to which it is the function of the Humanities to give definition, value, and character.

There is an almost constant urge for the tourist or transient in the mountain and desert West to photograph it, to arrest its awesome landscapes and eroded mountain scenery in snapshots of one's own. The same is true of the professional nature photographers as well, though—from the earliest days of photography, it has been visual history (I think of Jackson and Powell) to the present.

There is an irony buried in this fact, in arresting the slow geomorphic processes over millennia through the reduction into one immutable instant in the photo. Yet this may be at the root of the impulse to photograph such scenery, here, here, and here, again, again, and again. It is as if in the solid quality of the scene the photograph is already present. The illusion of the solid, unchanging, magnificently permanent landscape on which fugitive, changing, seasonal life-forms play out their ephemeral presences seems to make the scene *already* a photograph, or at least kin to the image we anticipate in the still photograph, in its illusion of a basic, static permanence.

In the modern world, the scientist is taking over much of the role of the unassailable spokesman for truth. Formerly this was the office of the priest and/or king, each of whom was the final arbiter in any given dispute, the oracle in human form. But since the seventeenth century, the scientist, as the spokesman for the leading edge of the empirical method, has been the truth-sayer. His objectivity is much the same as the purported selflessness of the priest or church divine, and of the royal sovereign, whose whole life was a personification of the state. "L'etat, c'est moi," said Louis XIV.

The curious continuity in this succession from king and priest to scientist lies in their common ability to change their minds and yet retain the faith and support of their followers. They are all three human in their fallibility and superhuman in their access to current truth and the models of it they propose for civilization's views of itself and its place in the universal scheme of things. All three are institutionalized: *the* king, *the* priest, *the* scientist, since their role as truth- and law-givers is in the name and guise of the welfare of all. At their best, they are not themselves, so much as they become figures in the course of history.

High-minded youths seeking rewarding careers may find unique opportunities by becoming research scientists. As such, they become representatives of the quest for truth in the face of which all are equal. Indeed, as a scientist anyone can become a representative of truth itself and therefore unassailable except by other scientists in the common quest for demonstrable truth, which we all give over to them.

There is a devastating parallel—a correlation—between the nuclear arms race, with its proliferation of weapons far beyond the capacity to wage war in the old style, and the exploding human population of the planet. The psychological motivation that has led to one is surprisingly similar to that of the other. If we see these two critical areas of abnormal growth in the light of their motivations, they become metaphors of the basic Faustian forces of creation and destruction that are the blessing and the curse of human endeavor.

On the one hand we celebrate and extend and defend our physiological agency as biological creators, as the continuing progenitors of our kind. On the other hand our technological capacities—one might say our technological imperatives, for it is somehow imperative for human ingenuity to forge tools and implements in order to perform our will upon the natural world—have led to the destructive power of nuclear holocaust. We are now the victims of these two forces of creation and destruction: over-birth and over-kill.

Those who defend "the right to life" are as shortsighted in their piety and as emotionally self-protective in the realm of over-birth as are those who support the continued production of nuclear weapons in the name of self-protection and peace.

In both instances, the unforeseen problems produced by waste may be the factors that force the human race either into glory or oblivion. The wastes of human life, of civilization, pollute and engulf the ecosystems to which all planetary life is tied, more destructively every day.

Waste is curiously tied to the notion of "progress" and "growth" in Western Civilization. It seems to be one of the operant imperatives for humankind. But this is only a cultural, not a biological, imperative—unless we continue to confuse the two in the blind production of human numbers and to deify for the sake of "the economy" a runaway consumer ethic.

Ironically, as I recall writing in *The Clam Lake Papers*, "a synonym for *economy* is *waste*." The former is based upon the latter. The more prodigious the economy, the more ungovernable the waste. The heedless proliferation of babies is, in most of the world, so obvious that we somehow look right past it, while showing concern for proliferation of civilized waste. The statements we hear from the technocrats telling us that the technology to control these wastes is available but that economic and political stalemates and foot-dragging prevent its use are perhaps real enough, but where does the production-and-control-of-waste cycle end? What kind of informed faith can possibly evolve and succeed—one that is not as blind as the faith that one or another of the gods worshipped on the planet will prevail on our behalf? It cannot be that equally blind faith that predicts this capacity to control human waste can go on apace while both the numbers of waste-producing humans and their ingenuity in inventing new ways to produce wastes through civilized economies continue to proliferate.

Perhaps more dramatic in the West is the problem of the disposition of nuclear wastes. It is not, in this instance, the product so much as the by-product that embarrasses us. Yet they are indisputably parts of the same bargain. And to cope with the disposal of the prodigiously threatening waste of the nuclear adventures on our beleaguered planet, we must come to think in time cycles that go so far beyond a human lifetime, a national lifetime, or indeed the whole history of humankind as we have customarily appraised it in what we consider historical terms.

An entirely new planetary sense of history is necessary to sustain life in the future. Our study of the past thus depends upon firm and active geological perspectives of time if we are to survive our own over-production of wastes—just as the numbers of biological over-production must project beyond the time of our own lives.

EPILOGUE

The Hawaii Episode

Thanks largely to the critical reception of *The Clam Lake Papers*, I received a Fellowship in Creative Writing from the National Endowment for the Arts. I planned to use it to work on the literary-musical novel I had started, based on my experiences in China, Burma, and India during World War II. Concurrently, my university awarded me a David P. Gardner Faculty Research Fellowship to further my trans-Pacific collaboration with my ex-student Naoshi Koriyama, now a poet-professor in Tokyo, translating the contemporary poets of Japan. The awards freed me from university duties—and, as I chose, from Salt Lake City—for full-time work on the projects. Both resulted in books published in 1989. These *Salt Lake Papers* were simply set aside and left fallow.

Thus, for seven weeks during February and March, late in the winter of 1985–86, my wife and I, while I worked at these projects, lived on the Big Island of Hawaii.

While I was there, the North American landscapes most familiar to me were submitting day by day to the severity of the American winter. Snow and ice covered the western mountains and the plains of the Midwest alike, all those family places from which I had drawn nurture and a physical sense of identity, those local settings in which my parents and the early events of my life had formulated my character—together with the Salt Lake Valley of Utah, which since 1966 had been my home. Fierce storms originating in remote areas of the northern Pacific Ocean swept from the frigid wastes of Alaska and

Canada, down from the Canadian Rockies of Alberta, across the
windswept ranchlands of Idaho, Montana, and Wyoming, the stiff,
frozen plains of the Dakotas, the stubble-fields and rigid woodlands
of Iowa, Minnesota, Wisconsin, Illinois, over the chill waters of the
Great Lakes, to drop more and yet more snow over New England and
the Northeast.

Basking in the sun on the leeward Kona Coast of the Pacific island
of Hawaii day after tepid day, it was hard for me to imagine the in-
continent weather on the continent—the rigorous winter—blasting
those familiar landscapes of the mainland. Yet it was occurring simul-
taneously with the warming sunlight and trade winds lulling me in
the mid-Pacific.

Still I could remember vividly enough winters in Chicago, where I
was born and lived through my boyhood, where the blizzards would
pack streets, yards, and alleyways with drifts shoulder-high and
higher. And around Clam Lake, Wisconsin, the adopted landscape I
used for the setting of *The Clam Lake Papers*, my snow-bound book
about winter in the North Woods. I knew that as I soaked in the Pacific sun, the Clam Lake deer were huddled in hollows, where many
of them would die in the severe and unforgiving cold, while the hi-
bernating bear slept under the frozen surface, its metabolism and life
processes slowed to a minimum. Such matters were hard to credit
there in the benevolent semitropic air of Hawaii, although, with others, I tended to gloat over the reports of winter storms roaring across
the U.S. mainland, where the tilt of the Earth and the composite elements of winter made life so fugitive and housebound.

But five surprising events during that otherwise balmy, even-tem-
pered, halcyon winter season in Hawaii were the stuff of revelation
and helped to direct the composition of this book—along with what
I like to consider the continental drift of my personal experience and
the conjecture it draws upon.

For my motive in spending those winter months on the island of
Hawaii was not merely to escape the restrictive world of snow and ice.

It was as well a purposeful retreat from my Salt Lake City self and environs in order to write without distraction, and to draft what my fallow years of observations and notes in the mountains and deserts of Utah had proposed earlier as a sequel to *The Clam Lake Papers*, to be called, naturally enough, *The Salt Lake Papers*.

The sojourn in Hawaii did give me time, but equally important it gave me some essential experiences and some indelible images that embody and illuminate all the writing I'd done previously.

In order of their occurrence, here they are:

The first was the merciless pounding of the Kona Coast by the highest, most powerful, destructive surf in a decade.

The second was my unexpected sighting of pods of great humpback whales just off that same coast but in calmer seas.

The third was my clear viewing of Halley's Comet, come round into our skies again after seventy-six years, and seen from that most advantageous, southernmost spot in the United States, the southern tip of the island of Hawaii.

The fourth image, and for me the most potent among the five, came from circling in a lone helicopter the fiery eruption of the volcano Kilauea and watching the live lava flow from its current cone down the rain-wet slopes and into the sea on the windward side of Hawaii.

The fifth event—anticlimactic only in the quiet, artificial process it offered for my consideration—was a visit to the algae farms newly constructed and operated on the bare volcanic shoreline north of Kailua, noted otherwise for the lavish fabricated vacation paradises catering to the world's wealthy, the exclusive resort hotels and hideaway havens of the northern Kona Coast of Hawaii.

Virtually every theme and consideration I had gathered for this book was thrown into new and fuller perspective by these unanticipated, curiously timely events during that lax working time in Hawaii. Not the least of these was the clearer realization that in the most comprehensive and universal view of history and of each individual living unit within its awesome narrative, all events, all things, are timely—timely in their own being and germane to the ways we conceive and experience the human dimensions of faith and fate.

BOOK TWO

Torrey, the Colorado Plateau, and the Colorado River

PROLOGUE

As soon as my family was settled in Salt Lake City, I had begun exploring the territory, on foot in the Wasatch Range, rising immediately to the east, and by car to more distant scenes. Often, my companion was my English Department colleague and closest friend, Kenneth Eble. Sometimes, he and I would take off together on short hikes or weekend getaways to camp or explore in remote Utah places new to us. It didn't take me long to find that the mountain, plateau, and red-rock canyon country of south-central Utah held a special attraction for me.

In the summer of 1968 I was invited by two young friends to join them on a backpacking trip to explore the then little-known Spring Canyon region of what a few years later became Capitol Reef National Park. At the time we were on the fringe of what was designated as Capitol Reef National Monument. One of my companions was employed by the Utah State Travel Bureau. The other was a graduate student active in environmental studies at Utah State University at Logan. We were an odd but compatible trio.

We backpacked up the dry creek bed through red-rock canyon walls to the small pristine spring (which has long since dried up and disappeared). We set up camp nearby, and spent the next two days exploring and taking notes for miles up and down the creek between the sandstone cliffs. We then packed back to the car (a VW van) and drove to Torrey Town and up the Boulder Mountain road, still dirt at the time, to where it crosses over Pleasant Creek, which runs down the mountain into Capitol Reef. There, it cleaves the Waterpocket

Fold to join the Fremont River (which in turn joins Muddy Creek, from the San Rafael Swell, and then becomes the Dirty Devil, which empties whatever water hasn't evaporated along the way in the dry desert air into the Colorado River, and so on).

Our big idea was to follow Pleasant Creek on foot all the way down the eastern flank of Boulder Mountain to where it enters Capitol Reef. From there, we thought, we could hike to where we could hitch a ride (which you could do in those more liberal days) back up to the van. We got as far as the steep cliff above Lower Bowns Reservoir before we gave up and climbed back to the van. Our explorations concluded, we headed two hundred miles north, back to Salt Lake City.

I had been engaged by and initiated into that marvelous landscape that, in retirement, my wife, Deborah Keniston, and I chose later to call home for most of the rest of our lives.

To help establish the setting and atmosphere of the house we built near Torrey, Utah, I preface what follows with a poem of mine, "The Curving Wall in Wayne County, Utah," first published in a booklet for Robert Redford's Sundance Resort and Institute in Utah's Wasatch Range.

THE CURVING WALL IN WAYNE COUNTY, UTAH

The stuccoed wall
we built around
our mesa home
is curved.

Inside the wall
the structured house
keeps human lives
rectangular.

The house's walls
make four-square corners.
The roof is nailed aslant.
The shingles overlap.

Outside the wall
encircling the house,
the planet Earth
completes its rounds.

The wall is there
to help us see
the global curves
beyond our sight.

Between the house
and curving wall
the captured earth
collects our footprints.

Outside the stuccoed wall
the seasons turn
and swirling winds
erase them.

Only the wooden gate
opening out or shut,
but always there between,
is straight.

THE PAPERS

At Salt Lake City I am in the world.
At Torrey I am on the planet.

⁓

The trouble with most of our dealings with the natural world is that we continue to treat Nature as a singular proper noun when we have come to understand it increasingly as a summary verb.

⁓

Living in retirement at Torrey, I occasionally have led writing workshop groups from Utah schools and Torrey's Entrada Institute into the marvelously eroded landscapes of adjacent Capitol Reef National Park.

We gather for initial effects and my introductory lecture at the Sulphur Creek's Goosenecks Overlook. There, we are hanging out over one side of the abrupt 300-foot drop of the canyon, looking across the chasm and down to the serpentine curving meander of the small but steady creek at the bottom. It is important to *see* and *feel* oneself a current part of the geological time and forces that have shaped the scene and continue, as visitors gawk and gasp, to do so in their own ways in our own time.

Those ways, I point out, are least of all the smooth down-grade surface flow of the creek that we can barely see at the bottom; but, rather, those current ways are the combined geomorphic work of moisture on rock, in all its modes—all the abrasive sculpting by the solids carried downstream, most dramatically by the roil of sudden flash floods, by the heavy rain and wind storms that lash the exposed sides, and by the seep of moisture in the fissures of rock, the freeze-and-thaw through epochs of season change…

…and, ahhh, all the constant drainage following the geomorphic Earth movements that, ages earlier, had uplifted the land, causing dramatic surface erosion in the sandstone layers of the Colorado Plateau.

Locally, we could see how this action eroded the tilt of the long monocline we call the Waterpocket Fold and—named for the huge dome-shaped formations that had interrupted the early western passage of explorers from the east just over a mere century and a half ago—Capitol Reef.

If the workshop group seemed sufficiently caught up by the scene and its expanding perspectives, I liked to hitch the drainage of what we viewed to the whole complex hydrology of what we've named the United States of America, draining us steadily into the endless oceanic cover of our aqueous globe.

To get under way: the Great Lakes, funneling through the St. Lawrence seaway, via the tumble and dash of Niagara Falls; from the three-river confluence at Pittsburgh; the wide, rolling Ohio River collections, merging at Cairo, Illinois, near the middle of what our shortsighted history named "the Middle-West"; joining with the even wider Mississippi, which had begun modestly in Minnesota and earlier was fed also by the Missouri, with its own source at the continental divide in the Centennial Mountains of Montana, and had been joined by the Platte River System that had drained from the east-central continental divide through Colorado, Wyoming, and Nebraska—all heading south to the deltas awaiting at the Gulf of Mexico; next, headed south through New Mexico and Texas, the fabled Rio Grande, also en route to the Gulf; and, farther west, by the Oregon–Washington coast, the great northwestern Columbia River System, gathering from seven states and a Canadian province, then surging through its gorge and on to the Pacific; and—in our place at that moment, right there before us where we stood—a minor tributary of the exotic Colorado, later to be joined in Canyonlands National Park by the Green River, itself fed earlier by the free-running Yampa from across a northern stretch of the state of Colorado and the middle Rockies—all later to be interrupted on its way to replenish the dammed Lake Powell, being joined there by the San Juan, which had drained through southern Colorado, northern New Mexico, and southeastern Utah; next, on into Lake Mead, in the meantime having sluiced through Arizona's Grand Canyon; then, released and reconstituted beyond Hoover Dam, to be spread over the vast irrigated furrows of California's Imperial Valley before, virtually depleted, it trickles its last, if any is left, through a dry sand spit at the portal of the Sea of Cortez, which empties at the southern tip of Mexico's Baja California into the Pacific Ocean.

The movement and confluence of our priceless waterways—like the circulating life-blood in our bodies, the veins and arteries of "our" Earthly domain.

I sometimes interrupt that panoply hydrology lecture to remark by contrast about northern Utah's singular, solitary, interior drainage sump—the Great Salt Lake, into which all surrounding water sources collect and settle, while none flows out.

Over the years, we, ourselves, became intimate with the surface flow of the major rivers of the Intermountain West, with long leisurely floats down the slower, steady stretches and then, when soaring canyon walls narrowed overhead, plunging into the chute and the surging, pitching dash through a mad whitewater run and on, to relax again through the next calm.

Our friends Ken and Linda Steigers, of Juliaetta, Idaho, initiated my wife and me early, on their private annual family rafting trips on the Snake and upper Salmon Rivers of Idaho. Then, on one of our favorite floats, on the surprisingly colorful Yampa to its confluence with the Green River at Dinosaur National Monument. With friends and small groups from Utah's Museum of Natural History, we ran the Green River's wild passage through the length of Desolation Canyon, and, finally, the classic rafting trip on the Colorado River through Grand Canyon. We learned first-hand what it meant to go with the flow.

Another ploy of mine that I sometimes pass on to writing groups that I take to Capitol Reef Park is to call attention to the greatly contrasting vertical, as well as horizontal, time zones to be conscious of in the landscape we are in. Most obviously, the first features the geological eons of time, mute, but inherent in the whole scene. One must get well past the customary touristy term "scenic," which is altogether too immediate, even comparatively cheap, and grossly inadequate to serve the need.

Linked to the rock-face and to the shag-bark of certain trees, and dependent, it seems, on only the mere *idea* of moisture, are the colonies of varied-color lichens, the basic life-form compounded of fungus and algae.

Next is the organic lifetime of the scatter of plant life in such barren, inhospitably arid rock and sand. That would range from surprisingly intrepid wildflowers and scarce grasses, along with more hardy but still stressed weed and woody low bush—all of which are vulnerable and dependent on annual and seasonal conditions being favorable. Next in life-length to the usually stunted or often decaying desert trees, the piñon and Utah junipers that end in desiccation and decay. Their time, set against the sense of geological sequence, seems more like our own, but stationary and more embattled.

Next, the organized time and life of the creature worlds of current insect, bird, and animal (except for ourselves), so efficiently hidden, mostly nocturnal, and self-protected, through natural selection, against the indifferent elements.

We struggle to eradicate "invasive species" in what we consider our own natural landscapes; yet we humans are, ourselves, the most persistent and disruptive invasive species on Earth.

9-13-96: Sunset Point with an Entrada Workshop

The skies are very changeable this morning. The clouds are cumulus, summoned from the southeast, not the customary direction in these parts. Some are white and fleecy. Others grow increasingly full and dark. From time to time, these take over the sun and turn the landscape below to shadow, the uneven line of the horizon to silhouette.

The play of sunlight and shadow over the mesas, cliffs, and clefts in the slickrock darkens frequently, giving dimension and depth to the latter. When the sun breaks through briefly, the brightness is clearly fleeting and warms me only momentarily. It seems a heroic but losing attempt to regain the day.

My thoughts about this interplay between sun and shadow, between light and dark, move on to the larger alternation of day and night, heat and cold—a series of the old dualisms, the ones that always aim us toward good and evil, life and death. But this morning, I feel myself too much a part of the whole scene. That cloud-coursing above is repeated here below. Sunlight and shadow are clearly alternations rather than alternatives, happenings and events in the weather's ongoing process rather than categories or states.

9-14-96: Off Sunset Point with Entrada Workshop

"How old do you think that juniper is?" I was asked.

"Well, I don't know," was my honest answer, "but a lot older than any of us."

It is only one of the many old junipers and piñons in the crumbling red-rock area we're in. Their trunks are wonderfully twisted and gnarled, testimony not only to their great age, but also to the long, sometimes torturous terms of their growth, persistence, and longevity. Each juniper, each piñon, young or old, telling the story, *showing* the story outwardly at least, of its existence to date.

At my advanced age, I feel a kinship studying the twists and turns, the heavy lines in the ridges of outer bark, the inevitable signs of weathering we both show in our outer aspects. To some, the strange configurations of these old, stunted, struggling trees suggest agony and suffering. To me, they say persistence, the advantages of hope, the wisdom of adaptation to circumstances. Their presence in this unforgiving, geologically bred landscape home says to me, "Stay the course; play your hand the way it is dealt. Accept, but persist in your innermost organic wish. Let the passersby see you as you are, for entailed therein is your whole life story, what you've been and what you've been through. What you have become. Be humble and steadfast in maintaining your pride; be proud in, somehow, knowing your humbleness. For a while, at least, you and your story can outlive your own life."

≈

I wake from a sound sleep suddenly, turn over and check the clock. 3:10 a.m. Damn. The good, needed sleep interrupted. Shut eyes, go back. Don't wake too much.

No use. My mind refuses. Will not "mind" my intent, but is alive and racing, thought tumbling—a race between place-images and unbridled sequences. I have some control over the former, but there is a strange shatter of the latter.

Eyes still shut, trying to relax my mentality and "fall" back into the needed sleep. My mind (or is it just my almost random, self-serving consciousness?) races on. I am wrestling with it, thinking: back to sleep / thinking can't get back to sleep.

What will serve? What will work? The old folk idea of counting sheep. In spite of myself, I "picture" it. Dumb sheep jumping over a fence. But no. It must be the counting, not the jumping, that should work!

But it doesn't work. They are two different modes in the race of my mind—the thoughts and the thinking I am trying to control, trying to control, trying to (language suddenly intrudes—words: erase/ de-race!). I am shuttling from the sense of the sheep in their motion to the mounting count of numbers that is supposed to cancel the thinking and slip me back to sleep. Doesn't work. Just wakes me more.

Try something nice and familiar of my own. Eyes still shut, my mind walking from the Torrey house out to the mesa "point" to the overlook scene—the walk I've done so often, knowing everything along the way to the over-view of Calf Canyon, leading to Capitol Reef formations, the Henry Mountains on the far horizon...

Damn. The wakefulness is confirmed all the more. All the items on the way—the path we've worn, the clumps of dry grasses to the side, the clearing between two piñons and the half-dead juniper with the rough-wooden bench that Deborah made, the huge mound of the ant-hill just beyond, on the way to the point. My mind is recounting not the motion of the sequence but, stubbornly, the items in the sequence. In effect, I am counting. The items are accumulating.

My mind jumps to the "fast-cuts" on television and in movies— more and more the nervous mode of tempting the viewer's mind to meld the frantic shatter of instantly seen-and-gone frames into some private sense of sequence. Used with effect particularly in commercials and highly dramatic "action"...Editing film, "movies"...stop-time effects...

No use. I am thinking, not absolving thought.

Try music. Improvise one of the familiar tunes I play on the piano. In your head. Voilà? It works! The flow is true to the imagined act. The rhythmic sequence is unbroken. Eyes shut, my mind—my imagination—plays the tune through, the music un-shattered.

No sleep now. Might as well open eyes and enter the bedroom world and the world beyond. And, yah, hold on to the thoughts and the thinking. Get up and turn on lights and the computer. Start turning it to language, sequencing words on the screen. Get up and write it down.

I like the wry jokes that authentic westerners tell about themselves—and others. The ones that begin like: "This sheepherder comes into a bar with his dawg…" The riddle the rancher (they call one another "cattlemen") tells outsiders he is showing around his spread: "Three guys out in a pickup doin' the rounds. Which one is the real cowboy?" Answer: "The one in the middle. One of the others'll have to get out to open and shut the gates."

There is the true story about the expressionist Utah painter V. Douglas "Doug" Snow, who lived in and painted the Wayne County landscapes for most of his life, quite comfortably absorbed among the locals, told so often that it has become almost apocryphal: An outsider, entranced by the landscape, asks a local if he knows of any land for sale and identifies himself as an artist. The local—I picture him studying his shoe-tops for a moment before looking up, constrained—says, "We already got us one of those."

Beyond the broad possibilities of amusement and pleasure, the human capacity for humor, as well as spontaneous laughter, is a learned but an instinctive capacity. Along with language, it devolves with the possibilities of comparison and contrast, of alternatives, of duplicities in the expected and the unexpected, of conceptual disparities, which the mind accepts as a mockery of analytical consistency. Thus, humor and comedy—even puns—depend on the metaphorical duplicity processed in the human brain (i.e., *mind*)—as does language at large.

The well-remembered, self-revealing comic routine of American comedian Jack Benny: A hold-up man, brandishing a gun, says, "Your money or your life." Long pause, and he repeats, "Your *money* or your *life!*" Another perfectly timed pause before Benny's wonderful harried response, "I'm thinking, I'm *thinking!*"

My Roland digital piano in our Torrey house provides good times for both amusement and musing at keyboard—quite different from this computer keyboard I write with. As an improvising jazz pianist who can't read music notation more than one note at a time, I play only "by ear" (i.e., not by eye; I play what I hear, not what I see). Unlike trained musicians, who are taught to count and give notes their metric values, I don't count. Instead, I follow out the tempos and rhythms I've set, and hope to be fluid, not florid, metrical, or piecemeal.

Thus, I surmise that there is an essential difference between writing (i.e., composing) notated music and reading music, compared with *playing* and *hearing* music.

If they have the talent, professionally trained musicians (which I am not) can do either—and both.

Rhymes are a curious instance of confluence in our vocabulary. The child, the poet, the lyricist, the rap artist, searching for sound and sense in rhythmic combination of rhetoric and rhymes, including "slant" rhymes, assonance and consonance within the tumble of

words called to mind, find surprising new meanings and implications
as they combine.

At one point, when assembling these "papers," hoping to enhance a
sense of order in their proposals, I thought seriously of labeling them
with such rhyming pairs. A number of them came readily. I played
with "Essays and Assays," "Articles and Particles" (with the variation
"Articulations and Particulations"), "Probes and Globes," "Simula-
tions and Stimulations," "Add Here" and "Adhere"...

It was—always is—fun. More pertinently, each new pair gave me
its own suggested sense of what I was attempting as the papers accumulated, as they hoped, with language, to (forgive me!) yearn to
learn and reach to teach.

I am hiking alone on the packed sand on an almost level, open stretch
of Grand Wash in the park, quietly attentive to the wonders of where
I am, how natural I feel, moving at my steady pace, two-legged, alternating offset arms swinging, rhythmically steady in that bright, otherwise still scene.

In the back of my mind, full of my easy stride, the interior, un-
sounded whisper of unbidden song sneaks in, takes over to match and
mimic, soundlessly, the physics and tempo of my easy stride. The silent song, improbably inane, un-summoned, unheard, but there, as
so often it happens thus, is that venerated old soft-shoe melodic shuf-
fle of "Tea for Two." To the regular accents of my alternating foot-
falls, the tune and its voiceless lyrics take over the empty but engaged
mind: "Picture me / upon your knee / with tea for two / and two for
tea / just me for you / and you for me / a-looooone / (four beats, four
steps) / nobody near us / to see us or hear us / no friends or relations
/ on weekend vacations / we won't have it known, dear / that we own
a tel-e-phone, dear... (four-beat pause for step-beats, while my piano
mind adds a touch of syncopation as I step around an uneven patch
of flat sand...)."

The whole tune, more ghost and idle mute accompaniment than thought, all the way through and again. My rhythmic human movement there, in the middle of Grand Wash, Capitol Reef, the Colorado Plateau, state of Utah, country of U.S., continent of North America, planet of Earth. Music by Vincent Youmans, words by Irving Caesar.

John Keats's odes are especially good to mull over regarding such things. I think here about the lines in his "Ode on a Grecian Urn":

> Heard melodies are sweet, but those unheard
>   Are sweeter; therefore, ye soft pipes, play on;
> Not to the sensual ear, but, more endeared,
>   Pipe to the spirit ditties of no tone

We should be aware of the metaphorical ambivalence and ambiguity in our use of the word "land" in references to "the law of the land" and other uses of "land" in place of "nation," or even of "country." Such usage is probably a holdover from "life, liberty, and property" in British tradition. It is a misfit and is misleading in modern USA. Our animal instinct to mark our territory directs our language and can get in the way.

In introducing the classically trained jazz pianist and composer Dave Brubeck, on his return from a world tour, an interviewer stated the popular notion that "music is the universal language." Brubeck, who was noted for his jazz compositions and improvisations with odd, syncopated time signatures, cordially objected. "Not so," he replied, "the universal language is rhythm."

~

Whatever computers and artificial intelligence can do in taking over "the humanities," they will fall short of producing creative human metaphors. Robotic intelligence can compare and contrast endlessly, and will do so with analogies that can be either logical or illogical; but the controlled complex ambiguity in the creative insights of a meaningful metaphor is possible only to the human brain for both the inception and meaningful reception of metaphorical ambiguity.

Simply put, the successful metaphor is a lie we knowingly can conceive, commit, and, for its implications, believe. What artificial intelligence will be unable to replicate may simply be the human capacity to *believe*—in the middle of which is *lie*....

~

A graph is a static visual means of quantifying the relationship of two contingent factors. Like the mathematical equation, it is another human device to remove time from the dualities of circumstance. It is an analytical means of division, displaying what is essentially to be experienced and understood data as confluence and metaphor.

~

When poet-professor Brewster Ghiselin, an elder colleague in the English Department at Utah, retired in the late 1970s, I inherited his popular course called "The Creative Process." No one else wanted it, but I was interested and willing. It was peculiarly Brewster's course. He had edited the book *The Creative Process: A Symposium* in 1954 and added the subtitle *Reflections on the Invention in the Arts and Sciences* in the paperback edition (1985) used in the course. I continued to use his book as the course text. The experience has helped to challenge and direct my own thought ever since. Some ramifications seem to have surfaced in these current notes to myself.

~

The idea of utter singleness, whether of a particle, atom, molecule, item, or self—or its cosmic projection into a monotheist God, Nature, or "the Universe"—is a fundamental, functional human illusion. Organic life on Earth eventuates, persists, and evolves through com-*bi*-nation: by duplicity. The idea of one's self is, itself, our base human metaphor. The use of language is both its cause and effect.

The instinctive use of language, with its metaphorical imperative, gives definition to the individual *self*. Thus, every human life becomes its own allegory.

The names we have given to the beginning stages of formal education of our children all indicate the priorities of language and number in training to become civilized humans—"reading and writing and 'rithmetic," as the old song goes, back when they were taught "to the tune of a hick-ry stick."

When I began schooling in the 1920s, my parents, born in the nineteenth century, called it "grammar school." Then, as I moved through the early stages year by year, we called it "grade school" ("What grade are you in?"), and the years were split into two semesters—like 2A and 2B. By the time I graduated from the eighth grade (there was yet to be junior high or middle school before high school), it had become—and remains—"elementary school." There is social history in those names—as there is in all names. And, indeed, in all language.

I've just now realized, with considerable bemusement, a parallel I blundered into with the Christian Bible—a volume also composed of two Books in one, an old testament and a new testament, separated by historical time and circumstance.

I am embarrassed, but not surprised, when I detect the stain of vanity in my thought. "Vanity of vanities," sayeth the Preacher in the English King James version of *his* Book. "All is vanity and the vexation of spirit."

"Time is of the essence," we say when there is need for hurry-up action. Formally, it is a legal phrase that sets a limit on procedures. But look at it again as a basic philosophical premise. It now seems to be a fundamental statement of our metaphysics—even our emergent cosmology.

The effect of the Digital Age on human language can be seen as either revolutionary or evolutionary, or, preferably—given an enlightened approach to the perpetual dualism in the ambiguities of choice—as both.

Take, for instance, the proposed disappearance of cursive writing from the primary education of children. The flow and inter-connectedness of cursive writing is giving way to the dominion of the keyboard and type. Words in the formal sequencing of thought are being reduced to the manipulation of separate letters. The manual act of writing words, phrases, sentences in the progress of palpable thought becomes the interstitial sequence of the single letters, of the alphabet. The shift from cursive connectedness becomes more and more the literary pointillism of print. In fact, children are not encouraged to write but rather to print.

Language is variously reduced thereby and tends to abbreviation in both speech and written forms. Clear indicators of the change are the growth of acronyms and the disappearance of letters, usually vowels, like in the standard abbreviations of texting—which, ironically, is an inversion of what formerly was the fully rhetorical sense of "text."

Something strange has happened in our casual, conversational give-and-take of opinion, along with what is established via the media in recent times as Q&A. It involves the vernacular responses of assent and dissent. We seem to have no difficulty in saying just "no," with or without a head wag or qualification; but assent is another matter. I hardly ever hear a simple "yes" anymore. Instead, every affirmative response seems to slide to some extreme, unconditional certitude that is, at least rationally, in context, patently false, being expressed as unassailable.

The "yes" substitutes are all what a grammarian would call "weakened intensives," from indiscriminate idiomatic common usage, in which the power and precision of a strong word are diminished. It is like what has happened to the once powerful and now throwaway adjective "awesome," which is now used to mean mere passing approval.

In place of "yes," the responder now reaches for "exactly," "really," "definitely," or "perfect," "totally," or the more patronizing "precisely"—or the most common overkill response that I hear, "*absolutely*." Perhaps that is the farthest reach from a simple, no-nonsense "yeah" or "yes."

We seem to need absolution, or at least to show utter conviction—or *closure*, another vogue term, popular lately for "completion" or, on our computers, "done," a wishful notion I am beginning to question.

I remember being struck, when I was a student studying the New England Transcendentalists, by Ralph Waldo Emerson's assertion that "there is properly no history, only biography." I think that was from his celebrated essay "History." It is an idea that for generations has been a kind of basic American testament.

The presumption of that perspective is clearly that "history" is the story of human civilization and is dependent upon the impact of recorded individual lives and thought recorded in language. This was obviously pre-Darwinian conjecture, clearly shortsighted in relation to our twenty-first-century growing knowledge of archeological pre-history and evolutionary biology. Yet it is still an attractive notion about "history" popular for contemporary multitudes.

Emerson's emphasis on the individual self as the subject and center of his mid-nineteenth-century world and social philosophy was, and remains, peculiarly American in its stance. As a student of American civilization and culture, reading (and "teaching") Emerson and Tho-reau at mid-twentieth century, I was quite won to their almost sacred devotion to the unique individuality of the human "self."

I have now lived and re-considered far enough into the "digital" world of the twenty-first century to see the fault lines and limitations in their stance.

A re-reading of "Self-Reliance," first published in 1841, reminded me of Emerson's deserved eminence and cultural importance in the young American democracy, but it seemed to me to have been quite overtaken by much of our socio-political and literary history over the century and a half since.

However, this was not so when I went back in my re-reading of Emerson to "The American Scholar," his truly prophetic address to the Phi Beta Kappa Society at Harvard in 1837. Surely, this must have been a vital link between the two that inspired the pent-up, not-yet-oracular Walt Whitman, who recorded, "I was simmering, simmering, simmering, and Emerson brought me to a boil." Once the twenty-first-century reader gets through the first page of obligatory rhetorical setting for the early nineteenth-century academic occa-sion, the address becomes remarkably prescient, filled with surprising foresight and insights for our culture that are still valid and now ripe. They are often presented in the memorable, highly quotable aphoris-tic nuggets that Waldo himself sought for and prized as "lustres."

Any "truth"—indeed, the idea of truth itself—is, for us, both singular and by *nature* plural, both subject/object, considered as fact and also as if, given its circumstance, infinitely repeatable (thus implicitly plural). The idea of truth is likely to be both desirable and intimidating, being both real and ideal, both attainable (finite) and unalterable (infinite).

In this regard, the quest for truth is perpetually challenging for the human archetype that Emerson in "The American Scholar" called "Man Thinking." That goes for me too, Waldo, since I consider myself a singular human while also being an instance of your abstract, composite, plural collective noun: Man.

The binary basis of the Digital Age is a turn of the pages of human history in the conversion of number and the computation of data into inevitable pairs. The halls of Philosophical systems have echoed through the ages with ideas of opposition and doubleness. In some respects, we have come full circle from the cosmologies of ancient Greece; from Heraclitus, the philosopher of flux; from Manichean and Zoroastrian polarities on through Spinoza's qualifications of classic Cartesian dualism to the ensuing literary philosophies of eighteenth-, nineteenth-, and twentieth-century Europe; from Hegelian and Marxian dialectics and Kierkegaard's either/or through Bergsonian *élan vital*, Sartre's matrix of existential choice, and, in American philosophy, Charles Sanders Peirce's logic as semiotic and the empirical pragmatism of William James—but the space-time Digital Age now takes us into the spare world of number-and-data itself.

Our own existence now apparently depends and advances on duples. We live our lives from biological conception and beyond in duples. It is in our genes, our DNA, our double helixes. Whatever claim we can make of uniqueness is the product of doublings and com-binations. The idea of my individuality wears a mask of oneness, but must recognize the necessity and validity of the same for others as well. No man is an island.

〰

I'm surprised to find that in the above sequence of dualistic philosophers in European formal Philosophy, I neglected the early nineteenth-century Arthur Schopenhauer. His premier place in my own early extra-curricular student thought may be detected occasionally here. I first read Schopenhauer, selectively but wide-eyed, at the impressionable age of sixteen, and have found a place for his metaphysics and esthetics (particularly in art and music) ever since.

More recently, I've come across a couple unexpected, but not surprising, earlier proponents of the dual basis of both physical and metaphysical reality in human affairs. They both, evidently, were precursors of a sort in their time to the binary processing now leading us on the data trails of digits.

One is Friedrich Engels's *Dialectics of Nature*, which he left unfinished in 1883. In it, he suggests some kinds of the dualities in natural process.

The other is Edgar Allan Poe in some of his opaque passages on intuition and inspiration in his rather phantasmagorical, wandering philosophical essay "Eureka."

〰

The idea of a single human life depends on the dual facts of beginning and end considered whole, as an interim, as one. We speak of "a life." We ask of the child or the youth, "What will you do *with* your life," not "during your life" or "while you are alive." Being seen as individual, a "life" becomes a noun rather than a verbal process.

〰

What about the enigmas in our thinking about birth and death—especially about death?

Well, to begin with, as instinctively linguistic animals, we give such unanswerable questions about life the special (spatial?) identifying (classification) name (noun) *enigma*. Right?

What follows in the mental process are birth and death, the two separate beginning and ending names (nouns) that encompass the idea of a human's span of time as "*a* life"—a special-spatial unit begun and ended in time but, much like the way we are apt to misconstrue the *continuum* of *space-time*, as a continuation of successive moment-to-moment units between birth *and* death. Thus, being rational about it, life becomes the "*and*" at the moving center of that teeter-totter key phrase.

But, we insist, isn't life more than that? Well, given language, perhaps and probably, yes it is—or may be. It (noun) becomes (verb), in "our" time, what we make of it.

⁓

Every culture invents its own creation story, putting it into words. The venerated Hebraic-Christian Old Testament offers a pretty good genesis account at its out-set, at least in the standard English translation. Not knowing either Greek or Hebrew, I fall dumb (mute, speechless) as well as dumb (unknowing, "out of the loop") regarding earlier versions.

In English, it becomes "In the beginning..." Then, it turns into the recounting of the human story (history), and there's little but trouble (and much gnashing of teeth) from that point on.

But look again at the opening text. It says "*In* the beginning...," not "*At* the beginning..." And "begin-*ing*," a continuation, not a start-up or "out-set" (a hyphenated word I chose, in context, with considerable care above). Okay. Good. Again it is both careful human designation (noun) and interpretation (verb implied) that create clear—even if ambiguous—meaning.

≈

Academic and popular gender studies have helped to establish the dual nature of humanity in the terms "history" and "herstory" as more than a mere pun and passing play on words. It helps greatly to turn the generic "man" from gender-free "I-thou" to "us."

≈

My daughter, Julie Lueders, who died abruptly from a pulmonary embolism in her home at the age of forty-seven, was one of the most natural persons I have ever known. Our Julie, the much-loved and respected, inventive, rock-solid drummer-singer, with an unfailingly rhythmical beat (yet somehow demure), holding the music smart and steady behind her all-female rock band, My Sister Jane....

Julie Lueders, co-hostess—with dynamic Babs DeLay—of Salt Lake City's popular KRCL community-radio show, featuring recorded contemporary women musicians and vocalists—the show they called, fetchingly, "Women or Nothing"—suddenly dead, and gone, while we, her parents, both lived on. So grievous. So *un*-natural. She, her*self*, had always been so natural. She was, we all felt, in everything she did, *a* natural.

But then, I remember that note stuck on the refrigerator door in the home she shared with her longtime partner, Ann Bolland, and their pampered family of highly individual dogs and cats they referred to as "the girls," the note that declared, simply, "There is no 'ought' in this house."

≈

That apparently offhand yet shrewd and potent title that my daughter gave her radio show: it is worth hanging around it for a while longer. "Women or Nothing." No matter what angle of approach you assume, it is worth thinking about.

≈

I'm pleased with the mute metaphor of *dance* in the common come-back remark "It takes two to tango." That makes it more than a passing wise-crack.

In the lexicon of successful serious satire, the difference between *clever* and *cleaver* is, simply, the letter *a*.

Here is a kind of cosmological evolutionary history of our Earthly humanity as comprehensively as I can let myself conceive of it:

CHAOS—our name for the idea of unconditionally inchoate disorder.

COSMOS—the name for ultimate profusion, with the initial semblance of order.

UNIVERSE—the name and concept for what, at the furthest reach, has unity by definition and thus the initial *sense* of order in cosmic profusion—making all further reduction of *disorder* "down" to:

THE NUMBER THREE—the last remaining digit of disorder.

THE NUMBER TWO—the binary basis of evolutionary process on Earth.

THE NUMBER ONE—the human mental reduction to, and projection of, unique individual identity, based in the experience of the single human *self* and matters of choice within space-time alternatives, in pursuit of order through continuously ambiguous circumstances.

We make an interesting contrast between the adjectives "new" and "current."

Something said to be "new" is designated thus as singular within its moment, in order to distinguish it from its implied singular opposite, "old."

Something said to be "current" holds the "place" of the noun it modifies without singling it out from the continuity it is part of. The image is that of the uninterrupted flow of a stream. The human mind can consider it either way. Or both!

Now that we have entered the Digital Age on both feet, so to speak, the partnership of the human mind with the natural evolution of life on Earth may be represented, if only for the fun of it, as a fateful game of existential tic-tac-toe, with alternating *X*'s and *O*'s entered in the game diagram's open spaces between its two pairs of intersecting crossed lines. As soon as a winning third-in-a-row *X* or *O* falls in place, that game is over and "done." That is, there has been a winner and a loser—a yes or a no. A choice is made.

But it automatically sets up a new pair of games, and we have to choose which one (or both?) of those to play. *Ad infinitum:* time and life as *et cetera*. Each single life *be*-ing lived as an integer—in spacetime, as a kind of punctuation mark—filling an *ellipsis*....

There is no *a priori* purpose in terrestrial life on Earth. But this does not mean that human life is purposeless. Rather, as humans experience their lives, they are composed of a constant confusion of intentions and purposes. And they are continuously being renewed and refined with projected possibilities, wishes, conflicted ideals, and instinct-related goals.

A sampling:

The goal of Language keeps becoming poetry.

The goal of number and counting is rhythm—and, adding sound, is, eventually, music.

The goal of bodily movement is dance.

The goal of competition is contest and domination. Or elimination.

The goal of education is understanding and full human agency.

The goal of hate moves through disdain and contempt to the elimination of opposition.

The goal of prayer is to subvert natural events through supplication to deity, and thus to divert the process we call "fate" into wish fulfillment.

The goal of science is the establishment of fact. If advanced through mathematics and computation, it becomes equation: balance and equivalence.

The complex goal of sexuality, when coupled with that of hope— and, potentially, with human emotional co-existence at large—propounds attachment, conciliation, and, at its best, *love*.

The goal of any human belief in a personal monotheist God is to attach all finite Earth existence to one's name for an un-Earthbound yet somehow connected and concerned noun, a singular, yet infinite, Deity.

We capitalize "proper" nouns—such as Utah, America, Asia, God, Nature, Earth, Science, Humanity, and each of our individual personal names (family and "given")—in order for them to be taken, in context, as totally composite and indivisibly Singular; and, at least normally, they are meant to be without duplication or plural.

The custom already can seem a rather antique practice in the Digital Age (digital age?).

The nature of the infinite in current human technology, as the common phrase puts it, has "gone digital." Or is it "viral"?

We depend on our *choice* of words to express—to ex-tract, to ex-pose, to ex-plain: to tell what we mean....And, with imagery and with metaphor, to show *how we mean.*

The goal of the active human mind is to discover, understand, and contribute in effect, within the dual, co-existent binary evolutionary patterns of Earth's space-time: both *separation* and *blend.*

Try once more:

The goal—or, if you wish, the purpose—of human life is to continue consciously to exist as the evolving human organism; that is, to confirm *self*-hood in the place-time of our humanity, and thus to persist at being the *noun* entity that furthers the predication of organic development in Earth time and life.

May we learn to say Amen to that.

So, at this late, penultimate stage of my long life, what do I believe in?

I believe in—and *with*—well, let's say, both the alternating and direct currents of all life on Earth.

And, more personally: I believe in—and *with*—poetry and music—language and rhythm, within the possibilities of their confluence in—and beyond—my own living.

The goal of the confluence of human language and human music is song.

The goal of human song is *opera.*

How accurate was the preternatural choice of "Song" in the title of Walt Whitman's prophetic mid-nineteenth-century opus "Song of Myself."

⸻

The number ten thousand (10,000) seems to be a natural number to which we could count with a mental sense of the individual units involved.

"I'll bet you ten thousand dollars," says the casual wagerer, sure of himself in congenial banter.

In the traditional folk idiom of Southeast Asian culture, a life is spoken of as "the ten thousand things."

Beyond ten thousand, we normally think in whole, rounded-out amounts, in which our sense of individual units is subsumed—and thus merely assumed—in the total figure.

⸻

In his long, distinguished career and series of hallmark books, the genial entomologist turned socio-biologist E. O. Wilson has persuasively utilized his lifetime study of ants and other socially organized "colonial" insect species to illuminate the instinctive social dilemmas of human society. In his bravely titled *The Meaning of Human*

Existence, he deals importantly with prime matters of human instincts. Allowing for complexities beyond what can be proposed within the strictures of the biological sciences, he calls for necessary collaboration from the Humanities.

Ever since I brought Professor Wilson to the University of Utah in 1988 to participate in the first of a series of dialogues with notable authors of natural history (his dialogue was with naturalist writer Barry Lopez), I have followed his lead in my own probes—at a distance, but as a kind of grateful acolyte. As a much-retired academic short of my dotage, I feel equally brave in taking up his invitation. We all need, and we must face, our challenges.

With due modesty, I confess that much—perhaps most—of what has been developing in the patterns of conjecture in these "papers" is my considered response to Wilson's call for perspectives from the Humanities. My hope is to keep the line of my thought always running parallel with the discipline of his scientist's insights.

Wilson's summary treatment of human instincts in *The Meaning of Human Existence* ignores—*avoids* is no doubt the more accurate term—two vitally important and significant instincts of our human species. One is human sex. While sex is, clinically speaking, clearly within the biologist's concern, in the human world it is so protean, as it spills over into all facets of the human drama, that his avoidance is wise. Even socio-biology alone cannot contain it. Leave it to the psychobabble of others.

The second instinct that Wilson leaves to others—and I am not alone in considering it fundamental—is the human instinct for, and with, language.

Practically, by definition, the Humanities are composed of, and disseminated by, language: Literature, History, Philosophy, Law, Communication, Speech, Rhetoric.

As a retired, recovering academic English teacher-writer-poet-pianist, I am vitally aware of what is emerging in our universities as "Environmental Humanities." Language itself remains my "discipline," my territory and concern.

Dodging all the hermetic theoretical perplexities and arcane jargon of the professional linguistic scientists, no matter how enlightened their flowering over the last fifty years may be, I choose to go at the living roots. I mean to approach human language at its most basically common functional role in human life.

The growth and use of language in human life is so familiar, so much the business of our "second nature," that it takes effort to think back to its physical basis—back to its physiology, first of all, as speech. For speech is expressed by the speaker into shared ambient air, *clenched in our very breath*, as variable sound waves, having been formed by what could be called *cunning* physical vibrations produced in the vocal cords, and expelled with variable force and further shaping through the gullet, throat, mouth, past tongue and teeth (and to some extent through nasal passages), to be then emitted as a complex of meanings to be audited by others.

It is almost ludicrous, and seems pedantic or frivolous, to describe language thus—as a function of human physiology. Yet that is what language, as speech—and consequently in the "second-hand" forms mirrored in our thinking and writing—*is*, at least as a significant part of the audible currents in the physical world.

The surprise comes in the realization that, through speech, one's language expresses mental processing by shaping and directing the rhythms in our breathing, combining both the physics and the metaphysics of—there is a wondrously useful ambiguity here—our human *inspiration* and our *aspiration*.

～

The versatility of our vocal cords and physics of speech allows expression of the full range of our moods as human animals, from growl and grumble to praise and song.

～

We struggle to define the nature of consciousness. Having given it that name, we propose that, like each human being—living as a *self*—consciousness is a condition rather than process—a noun rather than, in the active human *be-ing*, a verb.

Only in language do we split the two.

～

As the author of this ramble of thoughts that I am calling "papers," I should start considering how I might best bring them to a close. I feel the need for a summing up, or at least a sensible kind of packaging before I send them off on their own. A parting summation? No, too "pat." A final personal essay? Too chummy for all this abstruse stuff. A thesis? Too academic. Still, something more formal—a kind of wrap-up, but also a further contribution with its own character—a point of arrival for me, but perhaps of departure for others. A separate kind of *disquisition*—a rather nicely antique term left over from the eighteenth-century Enlightenment, but still in use. Somehow, I associate it with Adam Smith's *The Wealth of Nations*. Maybe. Sounds good, with a touch of up-dating irony there—from eco*nom*-ics to *eco*-nom-ics. Hmmm. As my mother always said to us, "We'll see."

But I do need to think ahead. That's also what humans do. We recall and review, but we think ahead. We plan, amidst.

≈

It is a mistake to try to understand consciousness as long as we approach and define it as a noun, as a condition. That holds it in place, as if static. But it is process and shares the nature of *verb*. If we must have a noun for the "state" we consider *consciousness,* a better working term might be *apprehension*.

≈

We live amid a constant welter of waves.

I am fascinated by the dual implications of all wave theories—and their illustration in graphs that turn oscillation inert and visible. By the nature of vibration, oscillation and waves themselves: necessary patterns of alternation in their continuity. Pulses. Impulses. Rhythms.

Sound waves. Radio waves. Wave lengths. Spectra. Color wheels. Light itself as it "travels." "Rays," we call it, when light reaches a surface and is reflected and refracted into our retinal color cones within the continuous range of the wavelengths we humans can register as color in the brain.

The wavelengths beyond our limited human capacity but still "there," as our digital mathematics can attest to—and thus name as metrical number. The back-and-forth dual movement of waves—even the substantial waves in fluid water, in the lakes, river currents, and oceans—and in the meteorological movements of the atmosphere and all ambient air. The confusions of ocean waves at their impact of sea with shore. Riptides and tidal waves. Up-and-down, in-and-out, ripples, peaks and valleys, all made visible and held in their continuity for us on the metered screen of the oscilloscope.

≈

The sports audience's "WAVE," performed by a large crowd in a surrounding circular or oval sports arena, occurs quite apart from the competitive game going on separately. Yet it is a composite group activity in which each individual contributes his or her part. The

WAVE is necessarily a cooperative, even democratic, event. Each individual must perform knowingly and responsibly in his or her own place at the right coordinated time—if the WAVE is to work. This game is the antithesis of, but occasioned by, the contest going on in the field, with its reduction to the efforts between two competitors (or "champions"). Cooperation in constituting the WAVE is especially attractive to children, being a kind of child's game engaged in cooperatively by all. The WAVE has no clear connection with the motives and competitive action of the contested game they have come, ostensibly, to watch.

Archimedes's Principle. Newtonian Physics. Quarks and quanta. Gravity (?). All, now, in the Digital Age, available to the human mind, reducible to binary number, sequence, data collection, and both nano- and macro-digital calculation and technological manipulation.

And *friction*—a kissing cousin of waves. Rapid alternation, surface agitation against a second surface, and what happens by the opposing forces of the two-way interaction. Heat waves. Fire. Electricity. What Walt Whitman, in his prophetic "Song of Myself," as I remember the phrase, called "original energy."

Advances in the Digital Age are processed on the limitless binary basis of alternating pairs, usually proposed as 0 and 1—standing, electronically, for "off" and "on."

This is, apparently, the parallel and equivalent in evolutionary terms of the on-and-off binary basic sequence of biotic chemistry in organic birth and death—you might say the basic process of not only human history, but also of the continuing procedure of all life (and death) events on Earth. This can be seen as a key to the process we call Evolution.

Over the centuries of Western Civilization, we have been taught Socrates's dictum "Know thyself." In response to our binary processing of this century's Digital Age, we may need to shift that edict to "Know thy *self*." We need to shift it from psychology back to epistemology. Can we learn and heed the difference?

Peel back all the layers of meaning and history, and human language is a matter of wondrously complex vibrations.

However slight or imperceptible, there apparently is a wobble in the measurability of all movement—perhaps cosmic, but at least in Earthbound time. In exact repetition. In the "perfect" circle (and the age-old unsolvable problem of squaring the circle!), and thus perhaps in circuitry itself. In orbits and orbitry. Mutation in the molecular spiral of the DNA double helix. In the idea of endless *alternity*....

Beyond the Heisenberg Uncertainty Principle, the mathematicians' fractals, the physicists' chaos theory and "observer effect," is there an operating basic principle of *imperfection*?

The wobble is close to home in the time of our lives on Earth, the rhythms of our circadian orbit, our days and nights. The Earth calendars must adjust, trying to even out the metrics—the months among the twelve—thirty days or thirty-one, and February short-changed. Leap Year.

The wisdom of the Navajo weavers, famed for the balanced geometric patterns in their marvelous rugs, purposefully weaving an imperfection into one corner of the rug, "to let the spirit out."

≈

A curious and time-ly coincidence (confluence?) in these papers today:

Yesterday's indulgence at my computer desk produced the above musings about my fascination with waves and wave theory. I'd had the binary action of vibration, oscillation, and waves taunting my mind for a run of days. It was time to learn what I would write.

Then: This morning, the news media were full of the experimental scientific proof of Einstein's mathematical theory that proposed gravity waves. Expectations are that this proof of their existence will have untold ramifications, not only in astrophysics but also in the paradigms of science at large.

≈

I wonder, as my human mind wanders through the evolving history of its thought, if the creative process isn't dependent upon two *flukes* in following the pathways of language and number.

One we call "co-incidence," or, better, a *conundrum*. A popular (and suddenly quite pertinent and useful) conundrum is baseball catcher Yogi Berra's famous "When you come to a fork in the road, take it." A conundrum, it occurs suddenly, is another name, in this context, for *metaphor*. In music we accept and enjoy the ensuing sequential doubleness as *counterpoint*.

The second *fluke* factor in the human creative process awaits in the pathways of number and computation. Curiously, but not inconsistently, we accept its irrationality also as a challenge to established, "proven" numerical systems. That factor is *mistake*.

≈

Having begun these Torrey papers with a place poem, it seems fitting to bring them to something like a close with a pair of poems about language and the powers of metaphor.

The first is my rather brash *envoi* "Your Poem, Man...," first published in 1968 in the collection titled *Some Haystacks Don't Even Have Any Needle*:

YOUR POEM, MAN...

Unless one thing is seen
suddenly against another—a parsnip
sprouting for a President, or
hailstones melting in an ashtray—
nothing really happens. It takes
surprise and wild connections,
doesn't it? A walrus chewing
on a ball-point pen. Two blue tail-
lights on Tyrannosaurus Rex. Green
cheese teeth. Maybe what we wanted
least. Or most. Some unexpected
pleats. Words that never knew
each other till right now. Plug us
into the wrong socket and see
what blows—or what lights up.
Try untried
        circuitry,
new
    fuses.
Tell it like it never really was,
man,
and maybe we can see it
like it is.

The second, "Winter Set," appeared first in *The Clam Lake Papers*
in 1977.

WINTER SET

The child in me loves
the snow falling
in the dark
outside.

The child in me fears
the snow falling in the dark
outside.

In me the child can know
the snow falling in the dark outside.

The child is
in me.

I am
inside.

EPILOGUE

The Disquisition: On Language, Number, and the Humanities:
An Epistemology for the Digital Age

In 1977, in *The Clam Lake Papers* (p. 53), I made an assertion that continues to prompt further thought in the Digital Age: "I assume that humankind—the human being—is instinct with language." I still like the ambivalence of "instinct" in that assertion, being either/ both noun and the actively conditional part of the predicate—the verb. The ambiguity is functional.

It is a commonplace that humans are distinct from other animals because of our use of language. Like anything that is commonplace, human language and our biological instinctive inheritance are fundamental matters in our lives that are too easily just taken for granted as givens. Two basic oversights result from the exceptionalist view of our humanity.

First is our tendency to ignore the animal part of our evolutionary heritage. We commonly, and culturally, bypass and ignore the basic role of instinct *as animals* in our human lives and ways. At best, we privatize it, and propose cultural taboos and public regulations through laws—both civil and religious—to deal with the instinctive needs we choose to control. When there are conflicts in our instinctive social selves, we depend on human laws to trump and modify natural laws. We do it with language. And then our language does it both for and *to* us.

Secondly, because it appears natural and gratuitous in human being, we commonly ignore what language is—or, better, *does*—in the metaphysically abstract processing of experience. We simply use and depend on it to cogitate and communicate. Yet, language is primary to our peculiar sense of identity, of individualism, and also, by extension, to our common or group humanism, i.e. to family, tribal and cultural identity, deistic religion, history, and to the notion of humanity itself.

NAMES and NAMING

Our stance in separation from animal instinctive behavior depends on separating life and be-ing into the two basic interacting linguistic modes: NOUNS and VERBS. Simply put, nouns are *spatial,* being representations of items and events, images and conditions, which can be given separable identity in both actual and virtual (i.e. mental) *place.* Verbs are *temporal,* representing physical and mental events in motion, in alteration or equalization, thus occurring in *time.* In this respect, the copula (linking) verbs (*be, become, is, are, was, were,* etc.) are "stop-time" verbs. They function rather like the "equals" sign in a mathematical equation, although they also can serve as the temporal fulcrum for condition and/or sequence and consequence.

In any case, nouns and verbs together are our basic linguistic means of dealing with the intrinsic dual confluence that we have come to consider (and name) the "space-time continuum." The dual use of noun and verb in language is somewhat akin to splitting (or fusing) the atom in molecular physics.

Baby talk begins with the personal name-identity nouns, then the appropriate active verbs—something like the "Tarzan talk" that Edgar Rice Burroughs gave his fictional ape-man (with a woman, his mate in the movies, as his instructor): "Me Tarzan. You Jane." And then "Tarzan go" and "Jane stay." The complexities of language and thought develop from there, nouns serving as both subjects and objects.

In human thought, which, in language, is dependent not on single words but on their grammatical interaction, reality consists in the ongoing combination of the two, nouns and verbs—or, better, what they represent in our mentality as "facts" (which, in most Western languages, like English, are isolated further and given separate spatial identity with the articles—*a, an,* and *the,* or *this, that, which, etc.*). We then can combine factual relationships rationally (analogues) together, when the image-ination is involved, to express the otherwise irrational, disparate, un-natural relationships that we propose effectively in symbol and metaphor.

We can separate and isolate the noun and its verb only conceptually, for each, alone, is inert and in-actual without the other combined, or at least implied—being related integrally somewhat like what in physics, as has been noted above, is called the "space-time continuum" (which by now, as a basic concept, has dropped its hyphen and become simply "spacetime")—or, say, in the polar opposites in a magnetic field, combined simply in the singular noun "magnetism," or the double helix in the genetic molecule of DNA. In traditional Chinese philosophy such dualism is pre-figured in the interlocking symbolic yin-yang combination representing wholeness and reality. This is what humans, as "thinking animals," do. Being "instinct with language," however, the human is reason-able and ana-lytical, but also metaphorical—able to imagine meaningful contradictions of facts and images with their corresponding expression in human language, which is, taken as a whole, a symbolic process.

All this is beyond just acting and re-acting, as all living organisms do. You could say that the "higher" orders of animals can "think" for themselves, while only human be-ings can also think *of* themselves. Thus, the notion of the noun "self" as one's unique and completely separable and virtually timeless identity is a peculiarly human idea. And language is its metaphysical technique.

The *noun* reflects our instinctive propensity as humans for individualizing through names and naming—including names for each of ourselves and others. Thus we appropriate, classify, and anthropomorphize everything in our world by assigning names, like our *selves.*

This extends to our stand-in personal pronouns and the all-purpose "it" for everything else, as well—and is basic instinctively to the developing human be-ing.

Because every noun, though abstracted from the living world, exists mentally in time as well as in idea in virtual space, language has partnered nouns with verbs to reflect motion, or change, as well as naming. Thus verbs are given *tense* to separate their differentials in time. Additionally, we use particularizing modifiers (adjectives and adverbs) along with the other "parts of speech" within systems we call, collectively, "grammar."

Owing to geographical separation and conditioned independence in their genesis throughout ages of our creature development, human languages on Earth of course differ in their grammatical particulars, just as they do in the physical phonetics, first as speech and then in the eventual distinct forms of writing and recording. But the need for nouns and verbs as the dual basis of any grammatical system appears to be species specific. So, too, is the instinctual mental capability we know as human thought and idea, of both analysis and metaphor, each of which can reflect and modify deterministic reality.

Language continues to evolve as the distinctive basic human social and intellectual tool. It is biologically instinctive in our capacity from infancy to maturity, as humans develop into human be-ing capable of complex thought and idea, of mental consideration and modes of communication. With the tool of language, we function actively aware of a current situation and experience, while also being active in memory with the abstract possibilities of both reason and imagination.

While rather idly considering the nature of number and numbering forty years ago in *The Clam Lake Papers* (p. 120), I wrote, "I wonder if the concept of *one* isn't the most unlikely of all numbering. It is probably a uniquely human device: the thinker separated conceptually from the thought—from *I* to *me*." In the Digital (binary) Age, the notion deserves further consideration.

Instinctively, with our innate need to name, we divide all occurrence (also by abstraction) into past and future. Importantly, in parallel with the peculiarly human identity of each unique, singular *self*, we commonly view life on Earth with the conceptual notion of time as a continuous series of singular, uniquely imagined present instants or moments, expressed in the common noun "now." This notion is given expression in the static combination of any two or more discrete occurrences with the adjective "simultaneous" and such phrases as "at once"—and is even implied in such common notions as "both" and "together." Einsteinian relativity confutes such notions.

The noun and our dependence on naming—the formal term is "nomenclature" and, for biotic classification in the natural sciences, "taxonomy"—are reductive means through language of proposing absolute identity. This is, apparently, a reflection of the human conception of the self as *one*—that is, a completely separate and unique identity. Like the unique number "1" itself, it is a fundamental construct of the human mind working *on* as well as *in* (that is, *during*) inevitable natural sequence and continuous *confluence* in the natural world.

All of what we call Nature on Earth exists only in time and thus is inherently binary. For us, that means "at once," both noun and verb collapsed into what we consider "one." Much of our difficulty in dealing with the natural world is that we continue to regard it as a single proper noun, *Nature,* while we increasingly come to understand it as active *verb.* The same can be said of the religious idea of the existence and the "character" of a monotheist deity.

As Heraclitus and his pre-Socratic followers put it, we never step in the same river twice. Theirs was a human metaphor for what the scientific method would approach as cause and effect, and for what our own age would re-define as digital—or, more accurately, as binary. For us, the common emblem of such functional paradox is the endless potential of binary identity—of converting naming from noun to number in the endless permutations of the barcode.

NUMBERS and NUMBERING

Conventional numbering by counting—naturally and physically, if not conceptually—is something we do by combining separate identities and sequencing them. We start with the notion of one, but we begin count-*ing* actually with *two*. We do not count to "1"; we count *from* "1". What we do with "1" is *cite* it. We could even say we *site* it, giving it a singular place as a noun.

But for any *one* to exist temporally in the natural temporal world, there must be at least an *other*. Except for the human mental abstractions of language—the insubstantial function of nouns and verbs and their refinements of systematic grammar (and the abstract mental manipulation of number in mathematics)—there is nothing else in, on, or of Planet Earth that is not subject to transience through combination, interaction, and change. The natural world, in which we have evolved as the dominant biological part, thus persists at base as binary. Along with language, our species is instinct with the concept of "one."

Actual, rather than virtual, numbering portends only with two. In "real time," existence is necessarily procedural. It is never inert and static—as is, for us, the noun and its human idea of any absolute isolation and identity; that is, in the idea of ONE. Thus nothing, except in human thought, can be functionally absolute—which would be absolutely singular. That would be stasis, an absolute noun without verb or plural, a lone datum rather than being functional statistically with others as *data*, rather than being simply event-ual. Isolate, pure one-ness, is pure human idea without function—except in the human concept of *one,* which has evolved along with the notion of the individually unique, gender-less material human *self* (or im-material *soul*), as in the neuter pronoun "one" for a hypothetical person.

The human story continues, vitally alive and distinctively cognitive, yet devolving in Earth-time, in which there is no irreducible "present" but only *confluence*, experienced in our terms of "now" and "then" within an evolving binary infinity of alternatives.

Only with the human notion of subdividing nature's binary process into the mental world of language—of abstracted names and activities, of noun and verb, taking us from percept to concept, and thus to precept—have we moved from nature's binary base and plurality to the singularity of the subjective "I" and objective "me," together with all of our projections of self into imaginary worlds of possibility and potential. And, it should be added, the pursuit of "meaning" and "truth" as singular terms in our linguistic models of existence.

It should be noted that this instinctive human notion of "one" is basic and necessary in our secondary "language," the world of complete abstraction: *number* and *mathematics*. That is increasingly our pathway to conceptual reality, leading potentially to infinite binary cosmology. In the place of our limited sense of *eternity* (and, in mathematics, *infinity*) we may be turning to binary *alternativ(e)*-ity—an endless duality that is perpetually actual only in confluence.

Our massive, perhaps endless, collection of and dependence upon data starts and stops (*interrupts!*) with the notion of "one" through all the mathematical abstractions in the confluence of digits, each of which is inert and inapplicable without human interpretation. This involves incessant choice. And that process (verb?) depends on what can be called the "metaphorical imperative," the instinctive human function of naming, plus the mental confluences we perform in the metaphysical abstractions of language, of thought, idea, premise, consideration, and—facing perpetual alternatives—of both instinctive and cognitive choice.

There is no "closure" in Earth's revolving, evolving spacetime. There is, rather, the furthering of Hegelian syntheses and furthering *dis*closure—and in our human *mean*-time, the instinctive devices of human language—our word games (like *these*), with which we combine human and natural history, with which we are able, increasingly, with our computers at hand, to count (*consider the dual meanings of that verb!*) and, while natural history proceeds (*with us as binary "units"*), to cope, to control, and to hope.